The Cheese Wheel

How to choose & pair

cheese like an expert

EBURY
PRESS

Emma Young

6

Ebury Press, an imprint of Ebury Publishing
20 Vauxhall Bridge Road
London SW1V 2SA

Ebury Press is part of the Penguin Random House group of companies whose
addresses can be found at global.penguinrandomhouse.com

First published by Ebury Press in 2023

www.penguin.co.uk

A CIP catalogue record for this book is available from the British Library

ISBN 9781529903652

Printed and bound in Great Britain by Clays Ltd, Elcograf S.p.A.

The authorised representative in the EEA is Penguin Random House Ireland,
Morrison Chambers, 32 Nassau Street, Dublin D02 YH68

MIX
Paper | Supporting
responsible forestry
FSC® C018179

Penguin Random House is committed to a
sustainable future for our business, our readers
and our planet. This book is made from Forest
Stewardship Council® certified paper.

To cheese! Well done for being utterly delicious.

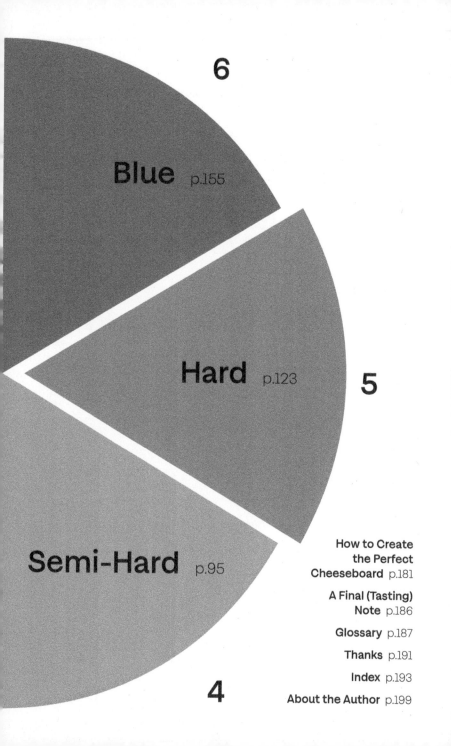

Welcome to
the Cheese Wheel

Every day I realise how fortunate I am to be working in a job that is also my passion. Being able to continuously learn about and share knowledge about what I consider the greatest food group is truly wonderful.

When I was at school, I didn't plan on working in the food industry and I certainly didn't plan on specialising in cheese. Looking back, there are many moments in my childhood which I don't consider having had an influence on my career choice, but perhaps these were subliminal messages throughout my youth, guiding me towards the path of cheese.

My parents owned a cheese shop and delicatessen when I was still a babe-in-arms, but they sold it long before I began eating solids. My Sunday family roasts would include a cheeseboard each week, without fail. To my horror – now I understand it, as a French speaker – my parents thought it would be funny to tell me to tell my teacher that I was *'fabriqué en France'*. Horrible people. But indeed, as much as I don't want to hear ANYTHING about it, apparently, I was conceived in France. As a child, my favourite book was an illustrated guide to French cheeses. I looked at it as a picture book until I could read, and then when I learned to read, we took it on our family holidays and I referenced it like a veritable cheesy trainspotter. Finally, going on two to three holidays per year to cheesemaking regions in France from the age of zero, really immersed me in the culture of cheese. I was eating Roquefort while others were eating *compote de pomme*.

Fast forward some years into my late teens/early twenties, and this is where my professional cheese career began. My undergraduate degree is in linguistics, which I studied at university in London, a city notorious for its expensive rent. While I was studying, I realised I needed a part-time job to fund myself in staying alive. I had just two criteria:

1. To work in something as far away from linguistics as possible (the course was intense, and I wanted to use a more practical side of my brain); and

2. To do something I truly enjoyed.

I had a think, and the thought process went something like this: 'Cheese. I really like cheese, maybe I should work in a cheese shop? Brilliant. Done.' And so, I applied for a couple of jobs at cheesemongers in London. I decided on a deli in Chelsea, as the alternative was a beautiful cheese shop – with the catch that they also wanted me to do waitressing. You do not want to trust me with your glassware. Sharp knives and cheese wires, fine, but the moment I hold a tray with glasses or crockery, it's only moments before I create the illusion of a Greek wedding. The deli was a *much* safer option. Soon, I became hooked. So much so that after finishing my degree, I stayed in cheese. For years I worked extensively in retail, then wholesale, with a bit of cheesemaking and a whole lot of judging and writing, before breaking away on my own in 2020 to create my own consultancy business. I now advise cheesemakers and cheese businesses across the world, from Bermuda to Saudi Arabia and Singapore, and back to my home in Kent, England. I teach cheese courses and influence all things cheese through my Instagram account, where I am known as The Cheese Explorer. I'm writing this book to discuss the best part of cheese: its flavour. We all know we love cheese, but what exactly do we love? This book will equip you with the skills to understand the basics of flavour in cheeses from around the world and to arm you with cheese vocabulary to guide you in your cheese-tasting journey.

HOW THIS BOOK WILL HELP YOU

Cheese, like any specialist food and drink, can be daunting. You are not alone if you have ventured into a cheese shop feeling out of your comfort zone. All the shapes, sizes, colours and smells, plus a team of specialists behind the counter, or a shelf in a supermarket filled with cheeses whose names have no meaning to you . . . it can be an anxiety-inducing experience for the best of us, when we're not familiar with the products. I know my first trips into wine shops early in my wine-loving journey were exactly the same. I was, however, younger and annoyingly British in those days, so I would say, 'I'm fine, thank you' or 'just browsing' in response to the lovely staff, then stubbornly choose a wine because it looked familiar or the label looked pretty, but I ended up hating it. I knew which wines I liked but I did not want to seem stupid in front of the experts. I have written this book so you can avoid these situations.

My aim is to make cheese more accessible by introducing you to the basic concepts involved when choosing, tasting, buying and pairing cheese with some bite-sized (pun fully intended) cheese information along the way. Cheesemongers are there to help you and they are extremely nice, I promise, but having a little guidance and prior knowledge before entering a shop will hopefully settle any fears and allow you to start your cheese-buying experience with a little know-how.

HOW TO USE THE CHEESE WHEEL

I have put together the Cheese Wheel to give you an understanding of the basics of cheese styles and to demystify their flavour. The wheel consists of six categories of cheese, based on their style and recipe. Some cheeses sit in multiple categories, such as Morbier being both a semi-hard and a washed rind cheese, and for these, I have chosen the most suitable section based on their dominant flavours. Next, I have put together four of the most common flavour profiles that you can find within each category. This is by no means an exhaustive list of flavour profiles, and you will find that most cheeses host a wealth of different flavours. Just as a wine may have dominant blackcurrant flavours and other fruits in the background, so does cheese. Batch variation of cheeses may also mean that a cheese tastes different one week to how it did the last time you tried it, so the flavours I have chosen are the most constant.

So, the Cheese Wheel is here to give you some common flavours as a foundation and, from that, you can build on your cheese vocabulary. I have then put together 112 examples of cheeses from around the world to illustrate these styles and flavours. Some of these cheeses will be familiar to you and others may be new. The Wheel will act as a reference for you to see how the flavours link together, to give you ideas for the next cheeses to try, and to help you better understand what you're tasting when you do. As you go through the Wheel, be bold – try new flavours and go out of your comfort zone. Or if you're looking for some comfort, learn more about the classics and rediscover old favourites. Most importantly, have fun. Cheese tasting should always be fun.

THE CHEESE SELECTION

When we think about the most popular and common cheeses in supermarkets, we can generally count their countries on one hand. Or one hand with a couple more fingers. The cheeses I have chosen come from over 20 different countries. Many of these cheeses are readily available and distributed worldwide, and some are a little more niche. In those instances I have used them to illustrate how cheese has long-distant relatives in flavour and style. Thinking texturally, there are only a finite amount of cheese 'types' which, if we HAD to, we could simply split into hard and soft. However, this would produce a Venn diagram whose centre (both hard and soft) would be as large as the two outer sets. I have chosen cheeses which represent flavour across the spectrum. Some are very simple, with just a few characteristic and identifiable flavours, and others change in every bite, like Willy Wonka's Everlasting Gobstopper.

You will hopefully find many of your current favourites in this selection. You may be surprised to see some missing – Halloumi, I am looking at you. The premise of this book is flavour and how cheeses are connected to each other via this medium.

In the selection you will find cheeses which date back thousands of years and some which have only been created within the last couple. There are cheeses which are produced on a large scale and some which are sadly close to extinction.

THE ANATOMY OF CHEESE

Before we head into how to taste cheeses, it's worth
familiarising yourself with three component parts of any cheese,
relevant to different flavour aspects. You'll see these terms
throughout the book.

RIND: The exterior of a cheese. This can be
natural, covered in moulds or washed. Some
cheeses don't have rinds – for instance,
fresh cheeses or those aged in inorganic
coatings such as wax.

PASTE: The interior of a cheese. No matter the
texture (soft in a Brie or hard in a Comté),
this is still called the paste.

BREAKDOWN: The cheese doesn't need a cuddle; this type
of breakdown is the area just beneath the
rind and into the paste. This is highly
desirable in certain cheeses, and it shows
both a texture and a flavour change which
we will explore in more depth with specific
cheeses in the Bloomy Rind, Washed Rind
and Semi-Hard chapters.

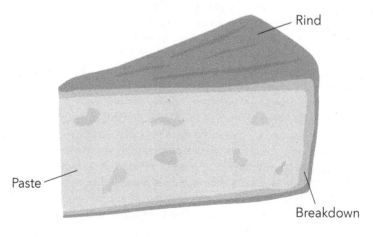

Rind

Paste

Breakdown

HOW TO TRAIN YOUR PALATE AND RECOGNISE FLAVOURS

I like to think about flavour and aroma in memories. This is how our brain processes them and this is how I remember them. Our olfactory memory refers to the recollection of aromas, so this isn't just me being a romantic. When I am analysing a cheese, I will frequently find a very specific flavour – an association from a past eating experience. For example, a Tomme de Savoie (page 100) which is fruity . . . but not just fruit . . . strawberry . . . but not just strawberry . . . strawberry laces. Specifically, the strawberry laces I used to eat every Saturday morning at orchestra rehearsal after three hours of practising the clarinet. Flavour is personal, and flavour is a lot about experiences too. Have you ever tried a cheese on holiday which tastes AMAZING, but when you bring it home to a cloudy January morning, it only tastes 'good'? Context has a large impact on the way you taste food.

Tasting involves focus and, if you are stressed, on the phone, working on a project or distracted in any other way, flavour becomes more meaningless and harder to identify.

Taste and smell are molecular senses. This means that when we are smelling and tasting, we are detecting molecules in the air (in our nose) and in our mouth.

When we smell a cheese, or anything for that matter, we are inhaling airborne, volatile molecules, which travel into our nasal cavity and are processed by two patches of sensitive skin in the front of our head. These volatile molecules are only a selection of molecules available in a foodstuff. Cheese can be complicated, so let's start simply. Let's think about a tomato for a second. When we smell a tomato, we are detecting the volatiles emitted by the tomato, not the entire tomato. A tomato will offer a mixture of volatiles, according to its DNA, proteins, sugars, etc. A tomato does not have a singular 'tomato molecule'; it is a mixture of molecules which come together to give us the familiar smell of tomato that we know and I love. When we smell a cheese, we are detecting aromas from the paste and rind. These vary considerably according to batch and producer variation, ageing room, mould growth, the feed the animals have eaten and many more variables. This is why cheese is so complex and why its aroma and flavour changes all the time.

When we taste a cheese, we are detecting more molecules. Our taste receptors are primarily on our taste buds on our tongue. When we taste a cheese, or any other food, we are allowing that food to interact with our taste buds. The flavour molecules in foods are dissolved in the saliva. When we are tasting a food, we are not just deciding whether we like it or not, although this is very important. We are extracting information from the food we have put into our mouth, to determine whether that food is suitable for our nourishment. You will see later in the book that I have explained more about why we like flavours, and this is linked to what the flavours may represent to us in terms of nourishment.

When I taste as a cheese judge, I need to focus. I sometimes pull myself away if I am tasting with a group. I occasionally close my eyes. I try to remove myself from any stimuli which may influence what I am trying to do. Sound is a huge part of this for me. I cannot taste in places that are too noisy. Do you ever turn the radio off in the car when you are parking? This is the same, but in cheese-tasting form. Taste involves concentration, and you need to make sure you are blocking out the outside world. Think meditative cheese tasting.

Of course, this is extreme and the *perfect* scenario to taste, but do not worry if this is not a state you can get into (or even want to) each time you put a piece of cheese in your face. Sometimes I do not want to analyse flavours, and that is completely OK. Sometimes it is good just to enjoy food without thinking about *why* you are enjoying it.

So, if you want to improve your cheese-tasting palate, the most important thing is to follow a few steps to get the maximum information possible out of a cheese.

TASTING CRITERIA

When tasting a cheese there are several criteria you can analyse. There are qualifications you can seek out and tasting models you can follow, such as the Academy of Cheese (which I currently teach), or Certified Cheese Professional, but I will show you the basics of these below. When tasting cheese professionally, we are looking at five different aspects, which you can also do at home with any cheese you eat. These are:

- Appearance
- Aroma
- Texture
- Mouthfeel
- Taste

(AATMT is not the most intuitive of acronyms, unfortunately.) If you have some cheese to hand, cut yourself a piece and go through the following steps with me. But first things first – eat a piece of that cheese. As a teacher and trainer, I always feel like I am setting my students up for failure of a very simple test when telling them to wait to taste the piece of delicious cheese in their hands. A percentage of my students will ALWAYS eat their cheese sample before we have started, like a guilty puppy. We are only human, and cheese is fabulous – so taste a bit of cheese first, enjoy it, don't think about it, and now that is out of the way we can begin.

APPEARANCE – How does the cheese look? What colour is it? Is there a rind? Can you see anything inside the cheese which may influence the flavour (e.g. truffles or fruit)? Does the cheese look OK? Our human instinct is a great thing, and you do not have to be a food expert to realise that sometimes a foodstuff may not be at its best. If it is slimy and green, then maybe it is one to discard. Is it a bit mouldy? Good! Mould is flavour and we will learn a little more about moulds that are good to eat within the following chapters.

AROMA – Does it smell much? Does it smell good? Does it smell like your teenage brother's socks? I hope not. Is there no smell whatsoever? The latter can be an indicator that the aromas are muted and could mean that the cheese is too cold. Does it smell like you are on a farm? Aromas can be very misleading. Washed-rind cheeses have a bark much worse than their bite. We will look at aroma more and see how it is linked to flavour, especially in the Washed Rind chapter.

TEXTURE – Here, we mean the texture of cheese to the touch. It should still not be in your mouth just yet. If it is, swallow, and grab another piece. Does it feel sticky, chalky, flaky or wet? When you squash it between your fingers, what happens? Does it crumble or fall apart, or does it form a cheesy putty? Manipulating a piece of cheese like putty releases aroma and flavour. It isn't the best look at a formal dinner party, however, so choose your audience.

MOUTHFEEL – OK, you have been very patient. Well done. NOW you can put it in your mouth. How does it feel? Is it bitty? Is it smooth and glossy? Does it have a nice bite to it? Mouthfeel is not a flavour or aroma, but it does add to the overall sensation and experience of eating a piece of cheese. Some detest the squeak of Halloumi, and some will enjoy a gooey cheese because of the texture, even if it doesn't have much flavour at all.

TASTE – All of the above stages have a huge influence on the flavour and enjoyment of the cheese. It is difficult to judge enjoyment by simply isolating the flavour. The above stages have such a big influence on the overall experience. Think about what you are tasting by starting with simple flavours and senses. Is it salty or acidic? Perhaps you know it is fruity but cannot quite pin down which fruit you are tasting. Does it taste like herbs? Has the flavour changed since you first put it into your mouth or is it still evolving?

Do not worry if you struggle to find descriptors when you begin your tasting journey. This is completely normal, and like with anything, the more you practise, the easier it will come to you.

HOW TO READ THE CHEESE PROFILES

For each cheese entry in the book, I have put together key facts and tasting information. Here's a little more on what is included in each entry:

Origin: This is quite obvious, but it's where the cheese comes from. Some cheeses are made or seen in several different regions or even parts of the world. You will see acronyms after certain cheese names, such as 'AOP', which stands for 'Appellation d'Origine Protégée'. This term, in short, means that the origin of the cheese and its processing is protected, and it cannot be made outside of that area. Further acronyms, such as 'PGI', will also appear and you can read about their specifics and the differences between a PGI and an AOP in the glossary (page 187).

Flavour notes: Cheeses will have all number of flavours, depending on their age, producer, milk type, time of year and other factors. For each cheese entry I have summarised the flavour in just three descriptors. These three flavours are those which appear the most frequently, characterising the cheese.

Pairs well with: Cheese with wine works for many but not for all. I have put together some wine matches as well as cocktails, mocktails, beers, spirits and non-alcoholic alternatives.

Milk treatment: Milk can be used raw to make cheese, or it can be heat-treated. I have used the terms 'unpasteurised', 'thermised' and 'pasteurised' here and you can learn more about their meanings in the glossary (page 187).

Animal: Here you see if a cheese has been made using the milk of a cow, goat, ewe, buffalo or a mixture.

Coagulant: This refers to the type of enzyme which has been used to split the milk into curds and whey. For cheeses which have been made using animal rennet, you will see the term 'traditional rennet'. The other coagulants referenced in the book are not from an animal and are therefore suitable for vegetarians.

Your next cheese suggestion: Here you will find a suggestion for a similar cheese to try next.

There may still be some terminology in this book you are not familiar with, so I have created a handy glossary (page 187).

Now that you're equipped with the professional approach to tasting cheese and are familiar with its fundamental components, you need to find the one you want to try first. In the following pages, I hope you'll find a few cheeses you're familiar with, plenty of cheeses you don't know yet, and many cheeses you'll grow to love.

Fresh

One

Fresh cheeses are perhaps the most understated of them all. They are young, with simple flavours and no ageing. They have had minimal-to-no manipulation and, in some recipes, they do not even have rennet or cultures added. One cheese in this section doesn't even use salt. Fortunately, this cheese is eaten extremely fresh and young, otherwise the lack of salt would be mildly terrifying as, in addition to adding flavour, salt is a very important ingredient for preservation in cheese.

Most of these cheeses are young and have a high moisture content, so they should be eaten fresh, as the name suggests. They are not stable and do not have rinds, nor have they undergone other processes which keep cheeses for longer, such as brining or extensive pressing. To this end, they do not travel well because they perish quickly, and are therefore not always seen outside of their native countries, regions or even towns.

When you visit farmers' markets around the world, you will often find fresh cheeses made by very small producers. The cheeses have sometimes travelled zero miles, and they often don't even have a name. There's something very exciting about a trip to the market knowing that there is a whole world of cheeses that aren't available at the click of a mouse or journey to a shop or supermarket.

Due to their simplicity, fresh cheeses can be made, and would have traditionally been made, in the home or in very small-scale production. This is how the first styles of cheeses were made – with minimal technology and equipment. This simplicity means you will see repetition in styles appearing across the globe, as there is not as much room for artistic license.

To start any cheesemaking process, milk needs to acidify. This is typically done with cultures (good bacteria) and rennet is then used to split the milk into curds and whey. If you've ever left milk in your fridge for too long, you'll see the bottle swell and the liquid turn into lumps or a big, semi-solid mass. This is the milk acidifying and curdling on its own. In modern cheesemaking, most cheesemakers use starter cultures to acidify milk under controlled conditions. Rennet is also added to most cheeses made under controlled conditions; however, this can be in very small doses, or the addition of an acid such as lemon juice or vinegar can be used to curdle the milk.

Some cheeses you will see in this book, such as Brousse du Rove (page 31) and Mascarpone (page 30), do not use rennet.

As we now have access to a wide range of aged cheeses, with a variety of flavours and strengths, we have lost the necessity and perhaps even the desire to eat some fresh,

Fresh

simple cheeses and so have repurposed many into recipes. Ricotta, for instance, is mainly used as an ingredient in recipes, such as pasta and cheesecakes, but it is one of my favourites to eat as it is, with a drizzle of good-quality olive oil or honey.

Fresh cheeses, then, are not the most commonly seen styles on a cheeseboard. Admittedly, the high moisture content and loose textures don't make for the most aesthetically pleasing cheeseboard choices, nor are they easy to cut and serve. But I love to put them there. Placing them in a ramekin or small bowl adds a new layer to a cheeseboard. Cheeses like Graceburn (page 25), a marinated cheese from the UK, or Xynomyzithra from Greece (page 26) make for a very interesting flavour starting point on a board and a great additional layer of texture and character.

The flavours found in the fresh cheese category are more limited than in the other chapters. As these cheeses are not aged and do not have rinds, they don't develop complex flavours. This by no means makes them boring – in fact, it is why I love them so much! As a cheese lover, it is common to be drawn to big, bold flavours to start. However, the more you taste, the more wonderful it is appreciating subtle nuances in the milk. It can be refreshing to taste a cheese that doesn't require thought in unlocking layer upon layer of flavour.

The fourth flavour profile in this chapter, 'Aged Fresh' is a little vaguer on the surface than the others. The term 'aged fresh' may seem to contradict the whole concept of a 'fresh cheese' chapter. However, these are cheeses which sit in this fresh cheese category in age and style but have then been yeast-ripened or aged gently to develop more flavours and to keep longer. It is interesting to see the contrast in flavour between differing age profiles of these cheeses, and this is a section that is very close to my heart – and stomach.

FLAVOUR
MILKY

As the main ingredient of cheese is milk, you may find this flavour profile a little obvious. 'Milky' is a subtle flavour, which is why it is sometimes overshadowed by others and why it is easier to spot in fresh cheeses with less complexity and fewer competing flavours. Milky flavours, however, do not come just from the flavour of fresh milk itself; there are chemical compounds called lactones which are responsible most of the time. These originate in the fat of the milk, and they are born when milk is heated.

It is important not to mistake fresh, young and milky cheeses as boring. It is incredibly skilful for a cheesemaker to make a subtle cheese taste good. As a cheesemonger, my favourite cheeses when I first began training were those with enormous, bold flavours such as Isle of Mull Cheddar and Roquefort (page 160). I did the same with wine (Sauvignon Blanc and Malbec) and beer (the hoppier the better!), as the flavours in these foods and drinks are easier to pick up on and identify. However, the more you appreciate a food or drink, the more you appreciate the subtle nuances and, in this case, the base ingredient of cheese – milk.

ORIGIN: Central and Southern Italy

FLAVOUR NOTES: Milky, sweet, saline

PAIRS WELL WITH: Feudi Di San Gregorio Greco Di Tufo
white wine or a tomato and basil water

Mozzarella di Bufala Campana DOP

(Unpasteurised, Pasteurised or Thermised, Buffalos' Milk, Traditional Rennet)

Mozzarella di Bufala Campana is a cheese that I cannot live without. My summer staple dinner is a caprese salad with this Mozzarella, fresh, home-grown tomatoes, a dash of sea salt, olive oil and not much else. A desert-island dish, perhaps?

It is a style of cheese called a 'pasta filata', translated into English as 'stretched curd'. Burrata (page 19), Scamorza (page 119) and Quesillo (page 21) are all examples of 'pasta filata' cheeses. To make this style of cheese, curds are immersed in hot water to soften them and to allow them to stretch. The acidification is very precise in Mozzarella-making in order to dissolve the correct amount of calcium, which allows the stretching to take place. When stretching, you are aligning the protein structure into strands, with pockets of fat and whey in between them. Imagine a tangled ball of cooked spaghetti which you separate and line up, but cheese.

'Mozzarella' as a standalone term is quite broad and is sometimes used to refer to stretched-curd cheeses made using any type of milk, and of varying, and sometimes questionable, quality. Mozzarella di Bufala Campana, however, must be made with fresh buffalo milk, processed within 60 hours from arrival into the dairy and it must use whey starter cultures and calf rennet.

When it has just been made, it has a tight elastic paste and an ivory sheen. It is milky, sweet and lightly saline, with the juices bursting in your mouth. After a little transportation we see the texture softening and a creamier paste coming through. It is best eaten incredibly fresh, with the greatest having never met a refrigerator.

Fresh

**If you like Mozzarella di Bufala Campana DOP, you'll also like
Buffalicious Mozzarella from Somerset, England.**

ORIGIN: Puglia, Italy

FLAVOUR NOTES: Milky, creamy, lactic

PAIRS WELL WITH: A sparkling, fruity white wine like a Trento DOC Brut,
or an American pale ale

Burrata di Andria PGI

(Unpasteurised or Pasteurised, Cows' Milk, Traditional Rennet)

Burrata. A cheese which seems to appear on every menu on the planet during summer. It's a cheese which still doesn't seem to have reached its peak nor lost its appeal in the restaurant scene. According to the Burrata di Andria PGI regulatory board, it has seen a sales growth rate of around 200 per cent over the last five years, which means it is not going anywhere. It is said that the person responsible for this viral cheese takeover is Lorenzo Bianchino, an Andriese cheesemaker who created this cheese in the early 1900s.

Burrata di Andria is the creamy bomb of a cheese that we all know and love, but with stricter regulations than regular Burrata, to ensure the quality is tip top. The cheese is essentially an outer casing of pasta filata cheese (like Mozzarella), fashioned into a sack and filled with Stracciatella, a mixture of shredded cheese and cream. When cut open, the insides fall out like a porcelain-white, cheesy evisceration.

It is a cheese whose texture and appearance also play important roles in the overall eating experience. The creamy mess has an indulgent appearance, and the mouthfeel completes this. Its flavours are buttery, with a welcome spike of lactic acid to keep you on your toes. These mild flavours combine well with fresh, sweet fruits and roasted vegetables, and the rich, fatty paste is cut nicely with the acidity of olive oil or tomatoes.

Fresh

**If you like Burrata di Andria PGI, then I would eat
as much as you like, as there is nothing similar.**

ORIGIN: Nationwide, India

FLAVOUR NOTES: Milky, sweet, acidic

PAIRS WELL WITH: White wines like Weingut Gunderloch
'vom Roten Schiefer' Riesling, or non-alcoholic drinks
like REAL Royal Flush Kombucha

Paneer

(Unpasteurised or Pasteurised, Buffalos' or Cows' Milk,
Acid Coagulation [Vegetarian])

Although I am far from vegetarian, you will often find me choosing Paneer-based dishes when in a restaurant. I love the texture and the way it takes on the aromatic flavours of Indian cuisine, flavours I struggle to replicate at home.

Paneer's origins are debatable, but evidence points to Punjab. It is widely used in the cuisine of Northern India and Pakistan. A large proportion of the population of India is vegetarian, therefore milk plays an important role in their diet as a source of protein. Paneer is now easily accessible in grocery stores and supermarkets around the world.

It is a very simple cheese recipe and one that you can try and make at home yourself. Paneer is still traditionally made in the home, simply by bringing milk to the boil and adding an acid coagulant (acidulant) such as lemon juice or whey, which separates out the solids. The resultant curds are then drained in a muslin cloth. To drive out more moisture, for a firmer-textured Paneer, the curds can be gently pressed under some weight. Buffalo milk gives a firmer texture; however, this is less widely available worldwide.

On its own, Paneer is a very subdued cheese. It is milky and slightly acidic. In the same way that you would perhaps not bite a chunk out of a block of tofu, Paneer is a cheese which takes on other flavours, creating a different experience each time. The drink-pairing suggestions above are to go with a typical Paneer dish, the tomato-based Paneer makhani.

Fresh

If you like Paneer, you may also like a well-drained Ricotta.

ORIGIN: Oaxaca, Mexico

FLAVOUR NOTES: Milky, sweet, salty

PAIRS WELL WITH: A Falanghina white wine, or a Bloody Maria (tequila)

Quesillo (Queso Oaxaca)

(Pasteurised, Cows' Milk, Traditional Rennet)

I spent some time a few years back as a cheesemaker, making (and eating) Mexican-style cheeses at an urban dairy in Peckham, south London. One of the cheeses we made was called 'Oaxaca', which was a recipe based on the Mexican Quesillo or Queso Oaxaca (originally Queso de Oaxaca, a name used outside of the region to illustrate that it is the style of cheese made in Oaxaca).

Many of my favourite cheese stories come from accidental creations, and this is one of them. The legend says that Queso Oaxaca was created by a young lady who was left alone in charge of making cheese in her household. She got distracted and, by neglecting the make, the cheese transformed into something different. She tried to rectify this by adding hot water and when this didn't work, she created a new cheese altogether.

If you have seen a cheese from Mexico which looks like a ball of wool, this is it. Quesillo is a pasta filata (stretched curd) cheese like Mozzarella. However, instead of being one large mass, once the curds are stretched into their long strands, they are kept that way, salted, and rolled into a ball. This is posh Mexican string cheese, and I adore it and its simplicity. I could not resist tasting the freshly salted strands in the dairy each time I was making it. You can eat it like this, peeling it like a ball of cheese string – this is my favourite method. It is used frequently in Mexican cuisine, including quesadillas and chiles rellenos (stuffed peppers) or it can take centre stage in queso fundido, a dish of hot melted cheese.

Fresh

If you like Quesillo, you may also like Mozzarella.

ORIGIN: Nationwide, Poland

FLAVOUR NOTES: Milky, sweet, tart

PAIRS WELL WITH: Prosecco Frizzante Extra Dry, or 0.0% alcohol-free cider such as Smashed Cider

Twaróg

(Unpasteurised or Pasteurised, Cows' Milk, Acid Coagulation [Vegetarian])

Twaróg is a Polish cheese also known as Biały Ser, Farmer's Cheese or sometimes Cottage Cheese. It is a very fresh, moist and crumbly curd cheese which is sold in a vacuum-sealed packet (unless you buy it fresh from the producer in Poland) to keep in all the moisture. It is a cheese which would have been made and still is made in people's homes and it is the result of a very simple curdling of milk and draining of curd. Twaróg is milky and sweet with a hint of acidity, generally from the acid used to curdle the milk. It can be used similarly to Ricotta in both savoury and sweet dishes, or simply sprinkled with honey and eaten as a breakfast cheese.

This cheese is used to make sweet pancakes called syrniki (or varškėčiai in Lithuania), a dish which is common to many countries around Eastern Europe. To make the pancakes, you mix this curd cheese with flour, sugar and egg and shallow fry it, making the most delicious breakfast pancakes. Serve these with a dollop of jam and an even bigger dollop of sour cream.

Fresh

If you like Twaróg, you'll also like Ricotta.

FLAVOUR
ZESTY

I am a sucker for fresh, zingy, sour and acidic flavours in both cheese and in cooking in general. I am half Filipina and, although I have been brought up in the UK since birth, I wonder if the flavours in Filipino-style cooking have had an influence on my palate. Perhaps that, or perhaps it came from my mum's unhealthy obsession with vinegar-soaked chips when she was pregnant with me! Taste preferences start in utero and the eating patterns of your mother during pregnancy do influence flavour preferences. When a child is born, they may show a partiality for certain foods that the mother ate while pregnant. This is firstly a survival instinct – knowing that these are safe – but is also due to the food's familiarity.

I am using 'zesty' here to describe the mouth-puckering, delicious sour and citrus flavours which come about in certain fresh cheeses.

The way these fresh cheeses are created leads to a wonderful acidity, which makes them great as a lift in cooking but also as a standalone cheese on a cheeseboard. These are flavours which remind you of citrus fruits with their fresh, vibrant notes. Some of these cheeses have an uncanny resemblance to the flavours of lemon and lime, which is wholly welcome.

Fresh

ORIGIN: Mainland and the Lesbos Prefecture, Greece

FLAVOUR NOTES: Zesty, citrus, salty

PAIRS WELL WITH: An Assyrtiko white wine, or a watermelon spritz

Feta PDO

(Unpasteurised or Pasteurised, Ewes' and Goats' Milk,
Traditional Rennet or Vegetarian Coagulant)

There are cheeses in this book which have been created within the last few years – and then there is Feta cheese. The cheese made by the Cyclops Polyphemus in Homer's *Odyssey* is said to reference the origin or predecessor of Feta cheese. I love the image I have created in my head of Polyphemus wearing a tiny apron tending over a vat of milk in his cave.

The name 'Feta' didn't come until the seventeenth century, and it is in reference to the 'slices' in which it is frequently presented and prepared before being placed into barrels for ageing.

Feta has a very moreish citrus acidity, which comes through from the milk used and the extended ageing time of two months. Therefore, you will find that cows' milk Feta alternatives are usually a lot more mellow, rounded and with less intensity. I very much enjoy the tang, zest and bite of a Feta PDO and barrel-aged Feta. Being kept in brine gives it a distinct saltiness.

I didn't jump on the social media trend of baked Feta pasta, but I understand why it became so popular – what an easy, rewarding dish filled with flavour and freshness from the cheese. If you haven't heard of it, the recipe called for any Feta to be baked whole in a dish with tomatoes and garlic, but the authentic Feta PDO must come from Greece, and it must be made from ewes' and goats' milk.

Fresh

If you like Feta PDO, you'll also like Graceburn.

ORIGIN: Kent, England

FLAVOUR NOTES: Tangy, herby, creamy

PAIRS WELL WITH: An herbal white wine such as Kamara
'Nimbus Ritinitis' Retsina, or an anise spirit like
Château 'KSARAK' *Ksara Arak*

Graceburn

(Unpasteurised, Cows' Milk, Traditional Rennet)

Hi, I'm Emma and I am addicted to Graceburn.

This is a relatively new addition to the UK cheese scene, having started its life in 2013 in a small dairy in south-east London. It is a cheese which I ALWAYS have in my fridge, and I break out in a cold sweat when I run out.

Graceburn is soft and a little crumbly, marinated in rapeseed oil with pepper, garlic and thyme. Cheese preserved in oil is commonly made in the Middle East, but Dave Holton, the cheesemaker, learned to make this in Australia, where it is known as 'Persian Fetta'. 'Feta' is a protected name used only for cheeses that come from Greece, but in Australia their naming laws allow them to call cheeses of this style 'Fetta', with two 'T's.

Graceburn has a bright, tangy acidity and richness from the milk, a distinctly nutty flavour coming from the rapeseed oil, and the herbs and garlic round this off and turn it into a meal on its own. As well as the original Graceburn recipe, it comes in two further varieties: a truffle version and a chipotle and lemon version.

If you can get past eating it out of the jar with a fork and want to know what else to do with it, you simply use it the same way you would use a crumbly white cheese. I find that it works on almost anything. My favourite ways to use it are crumbled over roasted vegetables (carrots or mushrooms in particular), a few pieces mixed into soup or on top of pasta.

Fresh

**If you like Graceburn, you'll also love Graceburn
with Chipotle and Lemon.**

Xynomyzithra Kritis PDO

(Unpasteurised, Goats' and Ewes' Milk, Traditional Rennet)

Xynomyzithra Kritis, a cheese name which would break a Scrabble board, is a soft, spreadable white cheese from the island of Crete in Greece. It is a mixed-milk cheese using goats' or ewes' whey or a mixture of the two. 'Xyno' means sour in Greek, which this cheese most certainly is.

To make it, whey is heated, stirred, topped up with a little whole milk and drained in moulds. Once salted and drained adequately, it is transferred into cloth and pressed to expel more moisture. It is then moved into barrels and stored for two months. I first tried this cheese several years ago and have been hooked ever since. I adore the zesty, acidic, and sour flavours which this mouth-watering cheese encapsulates well.

I like to have this on my cheeseboard, served simply in a ramekin. It is a great cheese to pair with seeded flatbreads. In Crete, Xynomyzithra Kritis is eaten in a savoury pie called *boureki*, which is made with courgettes and potatoes. It can also be used in salads and simply atop bread with a drizzle of olive oil if you so desire.

Fresh

If you like Xynomyzithra Kritis PDO, you'll also like Feta PDO.

ORIGIN: Highlands, Scotland

FLAVOUR NOTES: Zesty, buttery, tangy

PAIRS WELL WITH: Zesty whites like Villa Maria Private Bin Riesling, or a sparkling elderflower soft drink such as the one from Belvoir Farm

Crowdie

(Pasteurised, Cows' Milk, Nothing Else)

Crowdie has a very long history, with its production dating back to at least the Viking era – and some even say that it could go back to the Picts. The Scottish Highlands were cattle country prior to the clearances of the late 1700s, and every household would have had their own cow. The cream from the milk was used for butter production, and the remaining skimmed milk, after the cream was taken for the butter, would have been transformed into Crowdie. This milk would be set aside until it acidified and curdled. As a very simple lactic curd cheese, it would have had no starters or rennet added. The curdled milk would be heated and scrambled like eggs before hanging in cloth to drain off the whey. Salt would be added, and the cheese was ready to eat.

Traditionally a raw-milk cheese, Scottish regulations nowadays do not allow this, owing to the high moisture content and short shelf life. There are very few producers still making Crowdie using traditional methods, but even they must make it with pasteurised milk. There are variations on the original Crowdie, like Gruth Dubh (also known as Black Crowdie), which has cream added to make a richer texture before being rolled in pinhead oats and black pepper.

Crowdie's texture is moussey, soft and almost whipped. The flavour is moreishly tangy and zesty. It is frequently eaten with oatcakes and it is 'recommended' as a pre-game snack before a ceilidh (Scottish/Irish booze- and music-filled social gathering/dance) to alleviate the effects of whisky.

Fresh

If you like Crowdie, you'll also like real Cottage Cheese.

ORIGIN: Lombardy, Italy

FLAVOUR NOTES: Zesty, milky, acid

PAIRS WELL WITH: A fruity sparkling wine such as Mionetto Prestige DOCG Extra Dry Prosecco Yellow Label, or an alcohol-free sparkling drink such as NOZECO

Stracchino

(Pasteurised, Cows' Milk, Traditional Rennet)

Stracchino is a fresh cheese from the Lombardy region of Italy. Its name derives from the Italian 'stracca' meaning 'tired', which refers to the tired cows coming down from the mountains in the autumn. When the cows come down, their milk is very fatty and rich, and it is transformed into a cheese which has a texture not dissimilar to a young Mont D'Or (page 80) or a Venezuelan 'De Mano' – a curdy, tacky and sticky paste.

It is sometimes known as 'Crescenza', from the Italian verb 'crescere', meaning to grow. When it is left in a warm place, it increases in size like rising bread.

The flavours when young are simple, milky and slightly acidic, with all of these ramping up if it is aged for a week or so. You will not find it aged further unless you find it at the back of your own fridge.

My favourite way of eating Stracchino is as a filling for a *piadina*, a Northern Italian stuffed, unleavened bread. Stracchino and cured meats such as Mortadella are a popular filling, as well as typical bitter vegetables commonly grown and eaten in Italy such as radicchio, artichokes, and chicory.

Fresh

If you like Stracchino, you'll also like Squacquerone.

FLAVOUR
SWEET

Sweet flavours can appear in numerous different forms in cheese. Here, we are talking about sweet flavours in fresh cheeses and later in the book, we will discuss sweet flavours, such as caramel and butterscotch, in aged cheeses.

Milk contains sugar, the famous (or infamous) lactose. When you are making cheese, you acidify the milk. The acidification is the conversion of lactose into lactic acid. You may have heard that for people with lactose intolerance, aged cheeses are better, and this is true. The conversion of lactose increases with time, so the longer a cheese is aged, the less lactose it contains.

In these fresh forms, where the milk has been minimally adulterated, the sugars are more plentiful and easier to detect. The next time you are swigging milk out the bottle, or straight out of an udder, if you are lucky, think about the sweetness you are tasting. These flavours come out even further in certain recipes, such as the Ricotta and other 're-cooked' styles in this section. Sweet is a primitive flavour. A good cheese friend of mine once said that it reminds us of mother's milk, which is why we crave it.

The cheeses in this section can be eaten in a savoury guise, which is how we generally consume cheese, but they also lend themselves well to being enhanced with a little added sweetness (honey or sugar) and being eaten as a dessert or a sweet snack. Sweetness comes through in many cheeses, which you will see throughout this book; this can vary from sweet dairy to sweet fruit to confectionery sweet.

Fresh

ORIGIN: Lombardy, Italy

FLAVOUR NOTES: Sweet, creamy, citrussy

PAIRS WELL WITH: An Espresso Martini

Mascarpone

(Pasteurised, Cows' Milk, Acid Coagulant [Vegetarian])

Although it sits in the cheese aisle and we consider it a part of the family, its production methods are not typical of cheese. To make Mascarpone, milk is left undisturbed, allowing the cream to naturally rise to the top. This cream is skimmed off and this is what is used to make the cheese. The cream is heated, acidified using an acid such as lemon juice, and this in turn curdles the milk. No starter cultures or rennet are added into the milk to form this cheese (or not-cheese). Whey is drained off, salt is added and the cheese is ready for sale. On an industrial scale, to speed up this process the cream is separated using a centrifuge. As both products hail from the same region, some Mascarpone is made using the skimmed cream from Parmigiano Reggiano production.

Although we know that its origins lie in Lombardy, because it isn't technically a cheese, it is not eligible for a DOP status. Instead, the Italian government have given Mascarpone a Prodotto Agroalimentare Tradizionale (PAT), which recognises it as a traditional agricultural food from Lombardy. This does not prohibit its production anywhere else in the world, but no other region can claim its origin. Mascarpone at its best should be sweet, milky and slightly tart. It is the base ingredient of one of my all-time favourite desserts, tiramisu. It makes for a beautiful ingredient in savoury dishes also, stirring it through pasta, into a risotto or stuffed mushrooms. My all-time favourite snack using it is to get medjool dates, remove the stone and replace it with a big helping of Mascarpone.

Fresh

If you like Mascarpone, you may also like crème fraîche or Cream Cheese.

Brousse du Rove AOP

(Unpasteurised, Goats' Milk, Acid Coagulant [Vegetarian])

Brousse du Rove is something very special made in the south of France. 'Rove' is the breed of goat whose milk is used, named after the village of Le Rove, where they were first domesticated. They are a rare breed of goat, originally brought over by the Phoenicians, and this breed almost died out until their resurgence in the area in the early 21st century.

Their milk is used to make lactic goats' milk cheeses as well as this regional speciality. Brousse du Rove is made similarly to Ricotta. Whole Rove goats' milk is heated, a little vinegar is added in to acidify and curdle the milk, and the resulting curd is gently collected with a slotted spoon or sieve and placed into tiny conical test-tube-like moulds. The cheese is eaten fresh – only up to eight days from production and because of this, it is very difficult to find outside of its region. As if I needed another excuse to return to Provence again and again!

The texture is soft like a Ricotta, and the flavours are of pure, sweet goats' milk and floral, herbal notes. The flavour of Brousse du Rove is subtly influenced by each farm. As part of the AOP, the goats must graze outdoors and be allowed to feed on local vegetation in the surrounding wooded scrubland. The variation in flora on each producer's land is responsible for the idiosyncrasies of each local cheese.

Some eat it as it is, some with honey or sugar, or as a savoury version with olive oil. All are equally delicious. You can buy these from the farms directly or in farmers' markets around the region.

Fresh

If you like Brousse du Rove AOP, you'll also like Brocciu.

ORIGIN: Nationwide, Italy

FLAVOUR NOTES: Sweet, cereal, milky

PAIRS WELL WITH: A light white wine like
Vinho Verde, or a wheat beer

Ricotta

(Pasteurised, Cows' Milk, Vegetarian Rennet)

Although Ricotta is seen as its own entity now, its origins started, and its production still comes from, a waste product. It is made using the whey, which is commonly discarded after cheesemaking.

Ricotta means 're-cooked' in Italian. It is a second cooking of milk after cheesemaking has taken place. Milk is heated to the temperature needed to make cheese, cheese is then made and the remaining whey is then reheated to make this second cheese, Ricotta. Whey does not host the same components as whole milk, so you cannot make any type of cheese with whey. However, there are still proteins remaining in sweet whey after cheesemaking, and these solidify under high heat and after an acidulant such as lemon juice or vinegar is added.

Ricotta's origins are said to be so old that they are difficult to place, but most agree on Italy, and Sicily, where this really developed. Traditional Sicilian Ricotta is made from sheeps' milk, but we see cows' milk Ricotta far more commonly globally. Its flavours are sweet and milky and a little cereal (in other words, mainly reminiscent of digestive biscuits). Ricotta is used as an ingredient in many savoury dishes, but it also makes a mean cheesecake.

Fresh

If you like Ricotta, you'll also like Brousse du Rove AOP.

ORIGIN: Catalunya, Spain

FLAVOUR NOTES: Sweet, floral, milky

PAIRS WELL WITH: A fresh white wine like Txakoli de Getaria
from Bodegas Ameztoi, or a lemonade such as
Luscombe Sicilian Lemonade

Mató

(Unpasteurised or Pasteurised, Cows' or Goats' Milk,
Acid Coagulant [Vegetarian])

Mató is a fresh cheese from Catalunya in Spain. Although historically made with goats' milk (as cows were too expensive to keep), it is now more commonly made with cows' milk, but both types are still found on the market. It is a very soft cheese that looks and behaves like a Ricotta (page 32). Like Ricotta, it is also a whey cheese.

Like many of the fresh cheeses in this chapter, it does not travel much outside of its area, so it is relatively unknown, even to Spanish natives and Spanish cheese professionals, unless they have a relationship with this area. It is a cheese made without salt, and without this preservative, its shelf life is very short.

To make Mató, milk is boiled and then curdled with an acid like lemon juice or a little thistle rennet, from the cardoon plant found extensively in the area. Unlike its Italian cousin, however, it is used very differently. In the Ricotta section we discussed that it's used a lot in Italian cuisine. In Spain, fresh cheeses aren't used so much in their cooking – Mató is eaten as it is.

Mató is simple – fresh, clean, milky, sweet and a little tangy. This cheese has very simple flavours, especially due to the lack of salt.

It is most popularly eaten as a dessert with a little honey sitting atop – a dish called mel i Mató.

Fresh

If you like Mató, then jump on a plane to Catalunya!

FLAVOUR
AGED FRESH

'"Aged Fresh" is not a flavour,' I hear you say. Correct, it is not. This section is certainly the black sheep of the chapter. You will see throughout the book that I like to bend the rules, and this is a style of cheese I am adding into the fresh category, despite it not exactly being fresh. I'm doing this for the following reasons. In this section we are exploring cheeses that are made to a fresh or lactic recipe but have a little more ageing done to them. Lactic cheeses are cheeses that have been made using little to no rennet, which in turn sees a longer, slower production time that relies heavily on the acidification of the milk. When you add rennet into milk, the cheese is made much more quickly. So when you use very little or no rennet to make cheese, like with these lactic cheeses, the process is much slower. We commonly associate this style with goats' milk, like the Loire Valley goats' cheese Crottin de Chavignol AOP (page 36), but lactic cows' and ewes' milk cheeses are also delicious; you will see in this section that one of my favourite cheeses is a lactic cows' milk cheese.

In this 'Aged Fresh' selection I have also included yeast-ripened cheeses. These are cheeses which are predominantly ripened by *Geotrichum candidum* (a yeast), like St Jude (page 39). Their rinds are dominant in yeasts instead of moulds, the latter of which is found in bloomy-rind cheeses.

Aged Fresh cheeses typically exhibit flavours of mushroom, yeast and citrus. You can also find farmy notes, which many people love. However, this flavour is also the reason why many people really dislike these styles. As we find many a goats' or ewes' milk cheese in this category, we also find those 'goaty' and 'sheepy' flavours which some can find quite unpalatable. Some people really do have an aversion to this flavour, which comes from the fatty-acid composition of goats' milk and cheese. Two of these fatty acids are easier to remember than others. Caproic and caprylic acid linguistically sound like *capra/cabra*, which is 'goat' in Italian/Spanish. Unfortunately, '4-ethyl octanoic acid' just doesn't roll off the tongue as easily. There are many reasons why certain goats' and ewes' milk cheeses may taste more animal than others (including breeds and old milk), so it is always best to ask your cheesemonger for advice, or, if you are feeling brave, taste with your cheesemonger to find your favourite (or which you want to steer clear of).

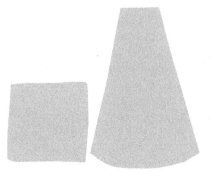

Fresh

ORIGIN: Loire Valley, France

FLAVOUR NOTES: Mushroom, zesty, earthy

PAIRS WELL WITH: Sancerre white wine like Henri Bourgeois
Les Baronnes, a lemon and thyme gin Cocktail or beetroot juice

Crottin de Chavignol AOP

(Unpasteurised, Goats' Milk, Traditional Rennet)

I adore Crottin de Chavignol. I spent a busman's holiday in the Loire Valley back in 2017, when I decided it would be a good idea to buy as many Crottin de Chavignol from different producers as I could find and to then spend the evening blind tasting. Yes, this is my idea of fun on holiday and, yes, it was all washed down with a healthy amount of Sancerre wine. Suffice it to say, they were all delicious and I highly recommend trying this out if you find yourself in that part of France.

My fridge is always filled with cheese, and I am on occasion guilty of leaving some for too long and finding them past their prime. Crottin de Chavignol is my trusty friend – it never seems to perish. It is great at ANY stage of its *affinage* – its refinement and maturing process – and, with its low moisture content, it ages well. It can be eaten quite young, but it can also be aged on further, until it resembles a geologist's discovery.

Its flavours vary between fresh, zippy and milky to more mushroom, earth and citrus (particularly lemon or lime) flavours. Crottin de Chavignol is best eaten as it is. The dense texture and complex flavours make it perfect to eat in small doses. If you get a younger version, it is great to cook as *salade chèvre chaud* – a salad served with grilled Crottin on toasted bread.

Oh, and by the way, its name means 'horse poo'.

Fresh

If you like Crottin de Chavignol AOP, you'll also like
Cosne de Port Aubry or Rocamadour AOP.

ORIGIN: Lot, France

FLAVOUR NOTES: Goaty, zesty, earthy

PAIRS WELL WITH: White wines like Château Tour des Gendres Cuvée des Conti Bergerac Sec, or a cocktail/mocktail with a rosemary twist, like an Old Fashioned

Rocamadour AOP

(Unpasteurised, Goats' Milk, Traditional Rennet)

Rocamadour is the tiniest of cheeses. It comes in the format of a small, approximately 60g flat disc. It is a snack-sized, raw-milk goats' cheese which has perfected the insanely difficult job of being well matured between the rind and paste while still exhibiting a giving texture. This is very tricky to accomplish with such a small cheese.

I had the pleasure of visiting the area and a Rocamadour producer back in 2018, and my goodness, the area is a culinary heaven. In this region of Lot, you will find walnuts, foie gras and duck preparations galore. These tiny cheeses are seen gracing every single menu in the area, appreciated as a starter – simply presented with a salad as an accompaniment and the occasional walnut. Rocamadour can be enjoyed young, with its moussey texture and fresh, lightly goaty and creamy flavours, or more aged and drier, where the caprine flavours are elevated, and a little spice greets you at the end.

A ridiculous number of these cheeses are made annually; approximately 1,000 tonnes are made and sold each year.

Fresh

If you like Rocamadour AOP, you'll also like Crottin de Chavignol AOP.

ORIGIN: Oxfordshire, England

FLAVOUR NOTES: Zesty, creamy, citrus

PAIRS WELL WITH: White wines such as Chapel Down Kit's
Coty Bacchus, or a Cherry Moscow Mule

Brightwell Ash

(Pasteurised, Goats' Milk, Vegetarian Coagulant)

Brightwell Ash is a new cheese made by Fraser Norton and Rachel Yarrow in Oxfordshire. They are new-age cheesemakers who had past lives outside of the cheese industry, and their cheesemaking adventure began in 2016. They make two goats'-milk cheeses, Brightwell Ash and Sinodun Hill. Their cheeses are vegetarian, using a coagulant made from a cardoon thistle. Cardoon is in the same family as artichokes. To make the coagulant, you steep the stamen in water to make a 'tea'. We will see thistle rennet again in the Washed Rind chapter, as it is commonly used in Spanish and Portuguese cheeses.

Brightwell Ash is a small disc coated in ash, which gives it its distinctive charcoal grey colouring. Let's talk about wrinkles. I love a wrinkly cheese. This is a shining example of a cheese with a beautifully vermiculated (wrinkled) rind. These wrinkles come from a yeast called *Geotrichum candidum,* which occurs naturally in goats' milk but can also be added into the milk to ensure optimum wrinkly goodness. Brightwell Ash and its sister Sinodun Hill are two of the best lactic goats'-milk cheeses in the UK, a style which you see more in regions of France, such as the Loire Valley.

In flavour, Brightwell Ash is zesty and tangy, like all good lactic cheeses should be, and a creamy texture envelops it.

Fresh

If you like Brightwell Ash, you'll also like Sinodun Hill.

ORIGIN: Suffolk, England

FLAVOUR NOTES: Creamy, lemony, buttery

PAIRS WELL WITH: Floral white wines such as Paul Jaboulet Aîné Viognier, or a saison beer such as Kernel Bière de Saison Apricot

St Jude

(Unpasteurised, Cows' Milk, Traditional Rennet)

It is hard to pick my favourite cheese, but St Jude is certainly one of them. I cannot visit a cheese shop or stockist without purchasing one. Fact.

St Jude is a small, lactic cows' milk cheese. It is based on a French recipe, but Julie Cheyney, who makes it, has added her own touch and uses raw milk from the herd of Montbéliarde cattle at Fen Farm Dairy. Julie set up White Wood Dairy in Hampshire, where St Jude was born. In 2014 she moved to Fen Farm Dairy, where she now uses the milk that is used to produce Baron Bigod (page 49), which also features in the Bloomy Rind chapter.

St Jude is a very slow make and an absolute labour of love. Unlike some very quick makes, the magic of this cheese takes time, including heading to the dairy at 2am to ladle the curds. The raw milk used to make this cheese creates a varying flavour and texture profile at different times of the season, with an influence from whether the cows are out on pasture or inside on their winter rations. The milk yield was enormous in December 2022, resulting in filled-to-the-brim cheeses just in time for Christmas.

When young, St Jude's flavours are fresh and lemony, with a light, feathered texture. When a little older, the paste breaks down beautifully, creating a whole new cheese with more vegetal and brassica notes.

Fresh

If you like St Jude, you'll also like Saint-Félicien.

ORIGIN: Aveyron, France

FLAVOUR NOTES: Animal, peat, wild

PAIRS WELL WITH: An orange wine like Tillingham
Qvevri Orange, or a cherry beer

Perail

(Unpasteurised, Pasteurised or Thermised Ewes' Milk, Traditional Rennet)

I hear time and time again, 'I don't like goats'/sheeps' cheeses. They are too goaty/sheepy.' While I think there are many cheeses which are mellow in their caprine and ovine ways, Perail is not one of them.

Perail is a lactic sheep's-milk cheese made in the same region as Roquefort. It originally came into being as a way to use up the excess milk at the end of a Roquefort make.

I'm not afraid to admit I occasionally struggle with this one myself. This is a cheese which immediately transports you into very close proximity of a sheep in a barn. Its flavours are intensely animal and barnyardy, alongside an earthy and lemony guise. I have, on occasion, tasted lamb chops and lamb fat in this cheese, but thereafter, there is an 'I'm-licking-a-sheep', lanolin quality that follows. The texture of Perail is wonderful. Young cheeses can have a slightly moussey texture, and once they are over this threshold – which is hard to come by unless you make or distribute it – they evolve into an unctuous, gooey sheep bomb.

Fresh

If you like Perail, you'll also like licking barnyard animals.

ORIGIN: Münster, Germany

FLAVOUR NOTES: Mushroom, vegetal, acid

PAIRS WELL WITH: A dry and unoaked white wine such as
Weingut Rudolf May Himmelspfad Silvaner GG,
or a Japanese Sidecar

Grisette

(Unpasteurised, Goats' Milk, Traditional Rennet)

Grisette is an ash-coated, lactic goat's-milk cheese made by Sabine Jürß. Her cheesemaking business, called Scellebelle, is where she makes not only Grisette but also a variety of other lactic cheeses.

All her cheeses are made with raw milk from her 60+ goats, which she milks by hand. She farms her land in Münster biodynamically, and this relationship with the land and the animals makes her extremely connected to the milk and her cheesemaking.

Her cheeses are set mainly with lactic acid and just a tiny helping hand from a small amount of rennet. Grisette is a cheese reminiscent of ash-coated Loire Valley goats'-milk cheeses.

The texture varies between firm and feathered for some and gently broken down under the rind for others. Flavours are typical of this style: a pronounced but balanced acidity, a little vegetal and mushroom coming from the rind and the ash coating, and some umami and savoury notes also.

This is a cheese which is best eaten as it is, although its flavours would lend themselves well to accompanying grilled vegetables like asparagus or courgette.

Fresh

If you like Grisette, you'll also like Selles sur Cher AOP.

Bloomy Rind

Two

Bloomy-rind cheeses are soft cheeses that have a white rind. These are rinds which have bloomed and blossomed like a flower. This sounds much more romantic in French, where this style is called *'croûte fleurie'*. There are several style variations within this category; however, they all have their white rind in common.

First things first – not every bloomy-rind cheese is a Brie. (Although, if it has a white rind, nine times out of ten, it will be in the same family.) A 'bloomy-rind' cheese is a term used to describe Brie and friends. When asking for this style of cheese in a cheese shop you can ask for a 'bloomy rind' or a 'Brie-style' option, and the monger will point you to the right section. What we do know is that these cheeses are creamy, salty and soft and this next chapter will show you the flavour variations within this category and what to expect when you taste them.

This bloomy rind is formed from the addition of a mould named *Penicillium candidum*, which is added into the milk or sprayed onto the outer surface of the cheeses when they are young. The most well-known cheeses in this category are Brie and Camembert, and, because of their fame and popularity, many other bloomy-rind cheeses are mistakenly identified as them. We will learn about the differences between the two later in the chapter, as well as discovering some lesser-known varieties from around the world.

Bloomy rinds are a type of 'mould-ripened' cheeses, as they ripen from the outside inwards, a process which influences both flavour and texture. The lactic acid (produced from the conversion of lactose in the milk) we mentioned in the first chapter is metabolised by many microbes – firstly by the yeasts, and then the moulds which grow on the outer surface of these cheeses. The moulds convert lactic acid (more specifically here, lactate) into carbon dioxide, oxygen and water, which bring down the acidity of the rind or, as we say, 'deacidifies'. Stay with me. The *Penicillium candidum* then metabolises the amino acids, a process which has a big influence on the flavour and texture of bloomy-rind cheeses. Or, in short, the white rind processes the amino acids, creating the characteristic flavours we find in bloomy-rind cheeses.

Ripeness can be affected by many factors but, principally, the older the cheese, the riper it gets. Other factors can influence this speed, such as temperature. If you keep a Brie outside on a sunny day, it will become runny. To identify ripeness visually, the best way is to look at a cross-section. Take your wedge of Brie and look at the middle – we call this the 'paste' (page 5) – and see how it looks. If you are struggling to handle it and it is excreting all over your hand, it is ripe. The cheese texture has changed, and we say, 'broken down'. If your wedge of Brie is firm and it looks chalky, then it is not ripe. Diehard cheese purists proclaim that a cheese MUST be fully ripe before you eat it, but I like eating mine a little underripe. This way you get both a mouthwatering acidity in the chalky heart as well as the gooey paste we know and love. Ripeness can hugely affect a bloomy-rind cheese, amplifying its flavour and, if pushed too far, cheeses can move into some less desirable taste descriptors such as pepper and ammonia.

Penicillium candidum can break down the fat in the cheese (a process called lipolysis) and, as these are generally quite fatty cheeses, a lot of this lipolytic activity can take place. One of the compounds, which is a consequence of this metabolisation, produces a mushroom flavour, which you will see later on in this chapter.

This category is the hardest to segment cleanly by flavour, as there are many crossovers. Bloomy rinds generally exhibit one or more of the following flavours in any one cheese. For example, a Camembert may exhibit brassica, saline and mushroom flavours all in one! So, here, they have been sorted by one of their most dominant flavours. These flavours may change further depending on the age of the cheese you are eating or the batch you have purchased. Cheese is a complex being!

FLAVOUR
MUSHROOM

Mushrooms, and in particular white mushrooms or champignon de Paris, have a very strong relationship with bloomy-rind cheeses. Their flavour is the calling card of *Penicillium candidum*, the main white mould we find on these cheeses. This mould has been selected and cloned for making bloomy-rind cheeses. We have created and conditioned moulds like this one to work with cheeses and, therefore, they only grow on cheese and not elsewhere. By selecting this single strain, which produces flavourful and bright white, aesthetically appealing cheeses, we've ensured that the mould has less genetic diversity, allowing for consistency and uniformity in the cheeses. These are desirable traits for widely distributed cheeses such as the AOP selections in this chapter. Brie used to be a greyish green colour before the age of *Penicillium candidum*! The champignon de Paris flavour is encouraged, and if you are trying the simplest of bloomy-rind cheeses, this is what you will find. In the more artisanal bloomy rinds, especially those made with raw milk, you will sometimes find porcini mushroom and even truffle flavours – and these develop with the breakdown of the fats in these cheeses too. There is a specific compound which arises from this process, named 1-Octen-3-ol, also known as mushroom alcohol. This is a delicious flavour profile I really enjoy and one I cherish when I taste it in a cheese.

Bloomy Rind

ORIGIN: Île-de-France and Lorraine, France

FLAVOUR NOTES: Mushroom, brassica, mineral

PAIRS WELL WITH: A Champagne like Goutorbe-Bouillot
'Champ de Craie' Brut Blanc de Blancs,
a Gin Sour or a green tea

Brie de Meaux AOP

(Unpasteurised, Cows' Milk, Traditional Rennet)

Brie de Meaux is the king of bloomy-rind cheeses. It is a raw-milk, bloomy-rind cheese made with very specific geographical and production conditions to make it utterly fabulous and a trendsetter for many cheesemakers around the world. 'Brie' is a bastardised name which we hear describing all types of white-rind soft cheeses. Like 'Cheddar', cheeses with these names can unfortunately be so far from the original that they are unrecognisable. Brie de Meaux is the French AOP cheese that many styles mimic.

Brie de Meaux is made in the east of France, in the regions around Lorraine. These cheeses are wide, flat and approximately 3kg in weight. The production of Brie de Meaux, although in large scale, is not fully mechanised – and this is what allows its flavour to shine. It is hand-ladled, dry-salted (not brined, which would be quicker) and aged on racks (naked, not in packaging or boxes) for weeks before it is permitted to be released for sale.

In a cheese shop it is easy for customers to slip into an 'Oh, I've had Brie, I'd like something more interesting', and this makes me sad. Classics become classics for a reason, and this is most certainly one of them. My Christmas board is NEVER missing a good, hearty wedge of Brie de Meaux, and I love the mushroom, brassica and mineral flavours which come through. The minerality in Brie de Meaux from certain producers can be reminiscent of oyster shells and seaside aromas, which can be fun. Unless you dislike shellfish, in which case I may have now ruined Brie de Meaux for you forever. Sorry. All the more for me!

Bloomy Rind

If you like Brie de Meaux AOP, you'll also like
Coulommiers or Baron Bigod.

ORIGIN: Suffolk, England

FLAVOUR NOTES: Savoury, buttery, roasted

PAIRS WELL WITH: Light Beaujolais wines like
Jean-Paul Brun Saint-Amour, or a Normandy cider

Baron Bigod

(Unpasteurised and Pasteurised, Cows' Milk, Traditional Rennet)

Many cheeses try to emulate others, and there has been a rise in the creation of new-age cheeses over the past couple of decades in the UK with cheesemakers creating new recipes based on continental recipes. Some are so far from the original they are unrecognisable. There is, however, no mistaking what this cheese is based on.

Baron Bigod is a textbook example of an artisanal bloomy-rind cheese. Its producers have used a combination of excellent milk and know-how to make a cheese which has completely won over the cheese market in the UK. It is made in Suffolk using Montbéliarde milk at its dairy, Fen Farm, on the Norfolk/Suffolk border. The cheese is not only a great example of a raw-milk, bloomy-rind cheese, but also a cheese which holds its ground, causing confusion when blind tasted against its French muse. Baron Bigod is a very well-made cheese, and its popularity and fame is ever increasing. Having started in a small dairy on site, it outgrew this fairly early on in its life, due to its popularity and success. While Baron Bigod production has moved into a larger facility, the original dairy is now used to make St Jude (page 39) and St Helena (page 102), smaller cheeses which are far better suited to this environment.

The flavours in Baron Bigod have a delicious range, making it a cheese to taste first with your cheesemonger where possible. Flavours range between savoury, buttery, mineral and brassica, all the way to a full-blown roast dinner. The texture is joyous, breaking down dramatically with age, becoming the runniest, most photogenic specimen.

Bloomy Rind

If you like Baron Bigod, you'll also like Brie de Meaux AOP.

ORIGIN: Haute-Marne, France

FLAVOUR NOTES: Mushroom, creamy, buttery

PAIRS WELL WITH: A fruity Merlot or a Belgian Tripel beer

Caprice des Dieux

(Pasteurised, Cows' Milk, Vegetarian Coagulant)

Caprice des Dieux is widely available in supermarkets across the globe. Its trademark blue oval box is striking, and it has a fairly long history, having been created in the 1950s by Jean-Noël Bongrain.

It spans three production sites in France: Haute-Marne, Mâconnais and Anjou. The company are very proud of their farming practices as well as of supporting their local areas. The milk to make the cheese is collected from a radius of 70km, two thirds of which is within 50km. They work closely with each farm to ensure the diet and welfare standards of the animals are of a high quality. The cows are out on pasture for 180 days of the year – and when they are indoors, their diet is based on rapeseed, clover, alfalfa and cereals and legumes. Each dairy farm has signed a Charter of Good Farming Practices, which has been developed with breeders and is audited every two years.

Its flavours are simple and people-pleasing. The cheese has a very typical bloomy-rind flavour profile of white mushrooms, butter and cream, with a hint of cauliflower also.

Bloomy Rind

If you like Caprice des Dieux, you'll also like Somerset Brie.

ORIGIN: Somerset, England

FLAVOUR NOTES: Mushroom, butter, saline

PAIRS WELL WITH: Oaked Chardonnay wines such as Liquid Farm
Golden Slope Chardonnay, a pear and honey cocktail
or a raspberry lemonade

Somerset Brie

(Pasteurised, Cows' Milk, Vegetarian Coagulant)

Somerset is a county well known for producing cheese, and a county made famous for its Cheddar. It has beautiful pastures which the cows graze on, so their milk is of a high quality. Lubborn Creamery, who trade under the name Cricket St Thomas, have been making soft, continental-style cheeses there for over 40 years. Milk for Somerset Brie is collected locally from partnering local farms in the West Country.

Flavours are buttery, creamy, milky and with the typical white-button-mushroom rind flavour I mentioned in the chapter introduction. The cheese is always perfectly ripe, and if you are looking for a giving texture and simple flavours, this is for you. Somerset Brie is a more neutral-flavoured bloomy-rind cheese, which makes it an excellent choice for toasted panini or as a melting cheese. It is very accessible in its flavour for those starting out on their cheese journey, and its yielding texture makes for a pleasant mouthfeel.

Bloomy Rind

If you like Somerset Brie, why not try Brie de Meaux AOP?

FLAVOUR
BRASSICA

Cauliflower is a flavour commonly picked up on in these styles of cheeses and I frequently pick up on cabbage and broccoli also. 'Brassica' is a somewhat poncey flavour descriptor, which I have chosen to cover a wider spectrum of flavours than one vegetable. It can cover you if you cannot quite put your finger on whether you are tasting a purple-sprouting broccoli or a Romanesco in your cheese. I blame my vegetable-gardening hobby, and my enormous love for bloomy-rind cheeses of this style, for my incessant use of this term. Brassica is a genus of plants, and includes the cabbage family.

One of the sources of these aromas and flavours come from volatile sulphur compounds, and these originate from sulphur containing amino acids. This is why you can really smell cabbage when a Camembert ripens, as the breakdown of proteins which turns the cheese gooey is also unlocking these amino acids.

The flavour can be incredibly pleasant when it is in balance, whereas sometimes, when overly dominant, it can be reminiscent of Grandma's over-stewed roast-dinner accompaniments. I love this flavour (brassica, not Grandma's overdone sprouts) and it is one of the most typical notes found in bloomy-rind cheeses, which you will encounter time and time again.

ORIGIN: Normandy, France

FLAVOUR NOTES: Brassica, truffle, butter

PAIRS WELL WITH: Pommeau de Normandie, amber ale or
Cawston Press Cloudy Apple Juice

Camembert de Normandie AOP

(Unpasteurised, Cows' Milk, Traditional Rennet)

I have been known, to eat a Camembert de Normandie like an apple on my train home after a gruelling month of Christmas cheesemonger shifts. Obsessed, one might say.

Camembert de Normandie is made in the north of France, in the Normandy region. A high percentage of the rich milk from the Normandy cow breed is used to make these cheeses. It is produced both industrially and on a small scale and, over the last few years, there have been several new *fermier* (cheeses made on the farm, not in a factory) producers of Camembert de Normandie joining the AOP. While the *fermier* cheeses are great and more traditional in their production methods, you shouldn't knock the larger producers, some of whom make some outstanding cheeses, sold by very reputable companies. The AOP ensures that the quality of the cheeses under the name Camembert de Normandie AOP are of a specific calibre and so artisanal and small-scale production does not always mean a better or more flavourful cheese!

In younger cheeses, you will find butter and mushroom flavours and as they age, and the texture breaks down, flavours become rich and buttery, filled with notes of mushrooms, truffles or cabbage.The aromas are very pungent when ripe. If you push them too far, they can go over this sweet spot and start to smell ammoniac and taste spicy. Many strong-flavour lovers very much enjoy this!

Bloomy Rind

**If you like Camembert de Normandie AOP,
you'll also like Tunworth.**

ORIGIN: Hampshire, England

FLAVOUR NOTES: Vegetal, truffle, mushroom

PAIRS WELL WITH: English sparkling wines such as Gusbourne Brut Reserve, or Freixenet 0.0% Alcohol Free Sparkling Wine

Tunworth

(Pasteurised, Cows' Milk, Traditional Rennet)

As discussed in the Brie de Meaux AOP entry (pg 56), there are many cheeses made which are replicas or homages to continental-style cheeses. Some are good, some are great but nothing like the recipe they have copied, and a few are outstanding. Tunworth is in the latter category.

Tunworth is a shining example of how pasteurised milk can make stunning cheeses. The milk used comes from a single herd, a few miles away from the creamery. The herd are a mix of Montbéliarde, Swedish Red and Holstein Friesian cows, giving a rich complexity to the milk.

This cheese, having grown from a production of 20 cheeses a day back at the start to around 1,600 cheeses a day now, is made entirely by hand. They have experimented with mechanisation of certain stages of the make, but the results delivered weren't as good as the manual. Each Tunworth is hand-ladled, hand-turned, and hand-wrapped.

Tunworth is not a shy cheese. Like a good Camembert, it has a bold character. Flavours range from cauliflower and vegetal notes to porcini mushroom and meaty funk. It is a perfect strong cheese for your cheeseboard or, if you want to be more creative, you can bake it in the oven, eat it melted over potatoes or bake it into a pie.

Bloomy Rind

If you like Tunworth, you'll also like Camembert de Normandie AOP.

ORIGIN: Northern France

FLAVOUR NOTES: Brassica, mushroom, vegetal

PAIRS WELL WITH: White wines like an Alsace Pinot Blanc, a Meteor Lager, or Stowford Press Apple Cider Low Alcohol

Coulommiers

(Unpasteurised or Pasteurised, Cows' Milk, Traditional Rennet)

Have you ever thought to yourself, 'I'd love to eat an entire Brie de Meaux AOP' but refrained from attempting to do so with 3kg of cheese? Well, Coulommiers is for you! At a mere 500g, Coulommiers is more approachable for this challenge and less stomach-cramp-inducing than its 3kg cousin.

Coulommiers is a relative of Brie de Meaux (page 48), with certain historical sources suggesting that it predates our more popular white-rinded friend. Coulommiers has many similar characteristics to Brie de Meaux, and many producers make both cheeses. As its size is much smaller, it ripens differently, and I absolutely adore eating this cheese when it is not fully broken down. It has a spritely freshness about it when young, with a mineral-water quality, zippy acidity and a whipped texture. As it ages, its flavours are creamy and mineral, with typical bloomy-rind notes of cabbage and mushroom. I find that it sits nicely between a Camembert de Normandie (page 53) and a Brie de Meaux, with a fabulous texture and rounded flavour.

Bloomy Rind

If you like Coulommiers, you'll also like Waterloo.

FLAVOUR
SALINE

Here, I am looking beyond salt and into the sea. I first remember identifying this flavour in bloomy rinds when I was working for Mons Cheesemongers. Each Friday we would taste, analyse and annotate our findings on 30 to 50 cheeses, so this is where my palate really had its workout and got buff. Tasting bloomy rinds would always give cabbage, creamy, salty and mushroom flavours, but there was something more applicable there that I couldn't put my finger on at first. I eventually linked it to oysters. Certain bloomy rinds give seaside, ozone, shellfish and seaweed flavours. I LOVE the sea and its ingredients, so finding this in cheese and not being repulsed by it out of context was amazing. When we looked at linking flavours to memories earlier in the book, I mentioned that this involves training your palate and this is why it took so long for me to make the connection. This flavour profile comes out hugely in French bloomy-rinds. When I was tasting these cheeses in different batches weekly at work, I often found a seaside salinity in certain bloomy rind cheeses. The flavour became so apparent in certain batches of Camembert de Normandie AOP that we started documenting the batch numbers carefully and figured out a correlation between the seaside flavour and a letter at the beginning of the batch code. The producer said that there were two separate cheesemaking rooms, which corresponded to two different areas of milk collection, with that one being closer to the coast!

I apologise if I have now put off any shellfish-allergy sufferers. This is merely a flavour link and there are no crustaceans present in the making of cheese! Unless you are eating Primula Cheese 'n' Prawns, where there definitely are some crustaceans therein.

ORIGIN: Berkshire, England

FLAVOUR NOTES: Saline, sweet, fruity

PAIRS WELL WITH: A sparkling cava reserva, or a tonic water like Fever-Tree Premium Indian Tonic Water

Wigmore

(Thermised, Ewes' Milk, Vegetarian Coagulant)

Early in my cheese career, I worked at Whole Foods Market in High Street Kensington, London, and this is one of the cheeses which absolutely stole my heart back when I was a wee cheesemonger baby. It is a bloomy-rind cheese – but unlike many, which are made with cows' milk, this is made with ewes' milk.

As it was one of my favourite cheeses and I was at the beginning of my learning journey, I asked the makers if it was possible to visit and see the cheese production. I had recently passed my driving test and, with a mixture of anxiety about driving somewhere outside my regular haunts and the excitement of seeing some first-hand cheesemaking, I nearly drove into a tractor in front of the makers who were standing outside to greet me. This was the first impression I gave Anne and her husband Andy. I'm both happy and slightly embarrassed to immortalise this in book form.

Wigmore is a smallish, round bloomy rind with a typical white rind. Although it's usually pearly white, don't be afraid if you see some coloured moulds appearing on the surface, and ask your cheesemonger for advice if you are unsure.

Wigmore's yielding texture comes from a technique of curd-washing where some of the whey is replaced with water in the cheesemaking process. The resulting flavours are salty with sweet milk, caramel, liver pâté, walnuts and more.

Bloomy Rind

If you like Wigmore, why not try Spenwood?

ORIGIN: Piedmont, Italy

FLAVOUR NOTES: Saline, creamy, fruity

PAIRS WELL WITH: A fruity red wine like Dolcetto d'Alba, a Japanese rice lager like Asahi Super Dry, or gooseberry soda

Robiola Bosina

(Pasteurised, Cows' and Ewes' Milk, Traditional Rennet)

Robiola Bosina is what I call a 'session cheese' – in other words, one I can eat in a single long sitting over an extended period. (Not quite the same method of 'eating like an apple', which I do with Camembert de Normandie and Saint-Nectaire). It is a cheese made by Caseificio dell'Alta Langa in the Piedmont hills of Italy. The producer makes many different styles of soft cheeses, which are their speciality. This one is a mixed-milk cheese using the milk of both cows and ewes. It is made by the same producer as La Tur (page 59).

It is a tradition in this area of Langhe to make mixed-milk cheeses. The location of the milking animals is remote, rural and riddled with trying steep slopes. It therefore has an economy based on small herds of cows, goats and ewes, and because of this, cheeses are produced in small batches and mixed together.

Robiola Bosina is a soft, square-shaped, bloomy-rind cheese with a very light, mineral, saline and creamy flavour. It has just a touch of an animal note, but it is gentle. The texture of Robiola is soft, like a Brie style which is starting to run. It is moreish and the salt in this cheese is nicely balanced, allowing for something I like to call 'sessionability'.

Bloomy Rind

If you like Robiola Bosina, you'll also like Mont D'Or AOP.

ORIGIN: Alba, Piedmont, Italy

FLAVOUR NOTES: Salty, creamy, zingy

PAIRS WELL WITH: A sparkling wine like Moscato d'Asti,
or a sparkling fruit drink like Shloer White Grape
Sparkling Juice Drink

La Tur

(Pasteurised, Cows', Goats' and Ewes' Milk, Traditional Rennet)

This is the only cheese in this book made from a mixture of *three* different milks – cow, goat and ewe. It is made by Caseificio dell'Alta Langa (page 58) who make over 20 types of cheeses including the Robiola Bosina (page 58).

You'd be forgiven for thinking that this is a cream-enriched cheese, with its luxurious, velvety texture, but I assure you it is just whole milk. La Tur has one of the most universally appealing textures I have seen in a cheese. In youth, it has a fine mousse and light, feathered soufflé texture; in adolescence, a giving, moist paste with a slight breakdown under the rind; and in age, a collapsed cupcake liner of decadent creamy goodness.

The flavour in this cheese is salty, with fresh milk, cream and a zingy acidity. The cheese is very balanced, which makes it easy to eat in session. What a delight!

Bloomy Rind

If you like La Tur, you will also like Brillat-Savarin.

ORIGIN: Rhône-Alpes, France

FLAVOUR NOTES: Salty, tangy, animal

PAIRS WELL WITH: A juicy red wine like Crozes-Hermitage, a semi-sweet mead, or a semi-sweet, alcohol-free cider

Saint-Félicien

(Unpasteurised or Pasteurised, Cows' Milk, Traditional Rennet)

Saint-Félicien is a real crowd-pleaser. It is based on the recipe for Saint-Marcellin, a smaller-sized cheese made in the same region, but is an adaptation. The story goes that a Saint-Marcellin producer was left with too much cream at the end of his day at market. He added this cream into his fresh whole milk so as not to waste it. With the enriched milk he made his recipe of Saint-Marcellin and, thus, Saint-Félicien was born.

Being enriched with cream contributes to its unctuous, giving texture. Its aroma is wholly reminiscent of the barnyard and animal aromas, which I mentioned when discussing Perail (page 40). The flavours are rich, milky, saline – and a little tang and acid come through if it is left for a while longer to age. I prefer to eat Saint-Félicien at a younger age, when it is light, fresh and creamy. Saint-Félicien is an indulgent cheese that needs minimal accompaniments: crusty bread and a glass of light red wine.

Bloomy Rind

If you like Saint-Félicien, you'll also like St Jude.

FLAVOUR
CREAM

Here, we delve into the category of added cream recipes. Certain bloomy rinds, with the unctuous and gooey textures that we love, have had a little helping hand to get that perfect texture. Most of the cheeses in this category have had extra cream added into their make and are not just made from milk. This process gives styles of cheeses called 'double' and 'triple cream', with Brillat-Savarin (page 62) perhaps being the most famous of them all. For the cheese and science nerds out there, there are neurons in our orbitofrontal cortex which respond specifically to the texture of fat in the mouth, hence why, even though these flavours may be simple and one dimensional, we LOVE them.

These cheeses are not my first recommendation for the diet-inclined, but as with all food, it is all about moderation! Added-cream cheeses are driven by a texture that makes us go wild and a flavour of rich . . . well, cream. I adore the contrast of the fatty, rich pastes and lemony notes that come through in certain cheeses. I also love the fact that there is practically zero thinking involved in eating these cheeses, as the flavours are tasty but not complex. Their flavours also lend themselves well to desserts, in particular when paired with fruits and berries for a tart and sweet combination.

Brillat-Savarin IGP

(Unpasteurised and Pasteurised Cows' Milk, Traditional Rennet)

If I had a pound for every time someone told me they love 'Savarin', I would have a fair few pounds. Sometimes nicknamed 'Savarin' or 'Brillat', its full name is Brillat-Savarin, as it is named after the 'renowned gastronome' Jean Anthelme Brillat-Savarin. This is a cream-enriched cheese with cream added into the milk, creating what we call a triple-cream cheese.

The production of soft cheeses, which are made from predominantly lactic curd, dates back to the medieval era in this geographical area. This slow cheesemaking technique was adapted to the pace of life in the Cistercian abbeys. It was then passed on to farms that undertook a mixture of livestock-keeping and mixed arable farming, where this unhurried task was easily seen to between other chores.

The addition of cream came in the nineteenth century. In the north of the geographical location where Brie is skimmed, surplus cream was available and, in the south, where cheeses were made with whole milk, cream was obtained from neighbouring regions.

This cheese is incredibly rich and dense, with a clotted-cream-like texture. The flavours on the rind are mushroomy and the paste is fresh and lactic when young, but develops warm, rounded cream and dairy flavours when further aged. These cheeses can sometimes have a reputation for being super simple in their flavours – however, there's a reason why they maintain a popular place in the market.

Bloomy Rind

If you like Brillat-Savarin IGP, you will like Humboldt Fog.

ORIGIN: California, USA

FLAVOUR NOTES: Creamy, mineral, zesty

PAIRS WELL WITH: A Grüner Veltliner white wine like
Veyder-Malberg Liebedich, a New England IPA,
or an elderflower tonic water

Humboldt Fog

(Pasteurised, Goats' Milk, Vegetarian Coagulant)

Humboldt Fog is a very distinctive-looking cheese hailing from Cypress Grove in California. With its bright white paste and signature ash line, it is visually one of the most famous cheeses from the USA.

It is a bloomy-rind goats' cheese with a very creamy paste. I love that this cheese was born in an irregular way – not an accident in this case, but a dream! Mid-flight, on her way back from visiting cheesemakers in France, Mary Keehn, the founder of Cypress Grove, dreamt about a cheese with a line through the middle. This doesn't have cream added into the recipe, but it really feels like it does, owing to the rich, dense and yielding texture. Its flavour is zesty, spritely and mineral when a young baby and, as it evolves and matures, this develops into a more rounded, animal and rich palate.

Humboldt Fog is an excellent ingredient for many a recipe. If you mix it with horseradish, cream and seasoning, it makes an outrageous steak sauce. Its flavour profile also lends well to desserts.

You can make Humboldt Fog brûlée for a showstopping dessert. Simply sprinkle on a layer of sugar and finish with a cook's blowtorch or under the grill to give a crunchy, sweet addition to this melted cheese.

Bloomy Rind

If you like Humboldt Fog, you'll also like Tomme de Chambrouze.

FLAVOUR NOTES: Creamy, buttery, rich

PAIRS WELL WITH: A sparkling wine like Louis Bouillot Crémant de Bourgogne Rosé, an IPA, or sparkling pear juice

Saint André

(Pasteurised, Cows' Milk, Traditional Rennet)

Saint André is a triple cream from Normandy, a region close to my heart. My childhood holidays were spent there, visiting D-Day landing beaches and spending rainy summers eating croissants out the boot of a car. Saint André uses milk from a 70km radius around the production facilities, ensuring that only Normandy milk is used to make the cheese.

It is a cheese that has, in recent years, been very successful in international cheese competitions, including winning a Super Gold Medal at the World Cheese Awards in 2021. Saint André is rich, indulgent, creamy and moreish. It is a savoury cheese that sits perfectly on any cheeseboard, but it also lends its flavours well to sweet treats and desserts. You can try pairing it with jams, berries and perhaps a nice coulis.

Bloomy Rind

If you like Saint André, you will also like Brillat-Savarin IGP.

ORIGIN: Normandy, France

FLAVOUR NOTES: Creamy, brassica, zesty

PAIRS WELL WITH: Light and low-tannin red Loire Valley wines, or a dry cider like Dunkertons Dry Organic Cider

Neufchâtel AOP

(Unpasteurised, Cows' Milk, Traditional Rennet)

Neufchâtel comes in many different guises. Six, to be precise. It is commonly seen around Valentine's Day in a heart format, when cheesemongers bring in this cheese specifically for its shape. During the Hundred Years' War, the cheesemaking ladies of the Neufchâtel became enamoured with their English occupiers. The cheese was consequently shaped into hearts for them to give as gifts. It can also be seen in bricks or rounds, but I am a romantic and love the history of the heart shape. Similarly to Camembert de Normandie (page 53), a high proportion of the milk used for its production must come from the Normandy cow breed (the beautiful cows with dark rings around their eyes, like mooing pandas).

When young, the cheese has a lactic, zesty acidity, a freshness on the palate and clean, simple flavours of cream and fresh milk. The texture at this time is loose, whipped and moussey. As it ages, it develops more of the bloomy-rind cheese characteristics we find in its cousin Camembert de Normandie. The texture becomes smooth and fondant-like, with more animal and cabbage elements coming through.

Bloomy Rind

If you like Neufchâtel AOP, you'll also like
Camembert de Normandie AOP.

Washed Rind

Three

Washed-rind cheeses get a bad press. They are the pit bulls of the cheese world, known for being offensively strong and unpalatable. Let's unravel some common misconceptions. These are cheeses that have had their rinds washed. In the previous chapter, we saw cheeses with bloomy white rinds created by adding moulds. In contrast, rind-washing promotes the growth of certain bacteria, which contribute to both texture and flavour.

We can thank monasteries and monks for many styles of washed and smear-ripened cheeses that exist today. There are several monastic orders across Europe closely associated with cheesemaking, namely the Benedictines, Trappists and Cistercians. One of the rules these orders followed from *The Rule of Saint Benedict* was that 'Idleness is the enemy of the soul; therefore, the brethren should be occupied at stated times in manual labour' for 'then they are truly monks when they live by the labour of their hands'. As monks were not permitted to eat meat, milk and its protein were a big part of their diet. With the vast lands they owned and the cattle which provided milk for them, they valorised the milk into cheese – a specific style of cheese that takes a long time and many processes to keep their idleness at bay. They would have stored these cheeses in humid cellars with ideal ripening conditions for the bacteria to grow. The cheeses would then have been washed to remove unfavourable surface moulds and, with alcohol then being safer to drink than the unsanitary water, they would have used what they had brewed to do this!

Washing cheeses does not involve immersing the cheeses in a sink and scrubbing them with a sponge and washing-up liquid. Washing cheeses uses a minimal amount of a washing solution – just enough to penetrate the cheese without drowning it or leaving too much surface moisture. Washing can either be with a salt solution (brine) or it can use the addition of alcohol. Beer is commonly used, as well as Marc – a distilled spirit from grape must. Époisses is a famous washed-rind cheese from France that uses Marc de Bourgogne, a spirit made from discarded Burgundy grapes. Washing can take place over several weeks with varying frequency, depending on the desired outcome and how the cheeses are behaving texturally.

Pink and orange rinds on a cheese counter will almost always be an indicator that the cheese you see has been washed. The washing alters the surface rind and creates the ideal conditions for bacteria such as *Brevibacterium linens* to grow. A strong odour follows suit – one that is somewhat bodily, and reminiscent of a school gym changing room. This is because these bacteria are the same as those found on our body – damp and warm conditions are the go-to for these chaps, which is why some washed-rind cheeses smell like socks. I have memories of travelling home after mongering shifts dealing with Munster and still being able to smell the cheese on my hands. No amount of hand-scrubbing made a difference for about two days . . .

Their bark, however, is worse than their bite. The aroma may be intense and off-putting, but the flavour is in a different league and, fortunately, not reminiscent of socks. The wash creates vegetal, fruit, savoury and farmy flavours. In washed-rind cheeses I enjoy the flavours of broth, meat, game, sweet fruit and more. You'll be surprised how approachable these flavours can be, so give one a go next time you're buying some cheese.

FLAVOUR
VEGETAL

These washed-rind cheeses are different to the most pungent, gooey, stinky-socks numbers. They are a little more restrained in their bodily aromas and flavours, and have more of a plant vibe happening. I'll split my examples into two distinct styles, for ease.

Firstly, there is a style of cheese from Extremadura in Spain, and over the border into Portugal, called the 'Torta' style. These are very soft cheeses that are difficult to cut and portion – instead, you cut off the top and scoop out their insides. They are made using a thistle coagulant which, being a plant, makes these cheeses vegetarian. We touched upon this type of coagulant when looking at Brightwell Ash (page 38). The thistle pistils are steeped and brewed, then used to separate the curds from the whey. The enzymes within cut the protein chains at a different place than animal rennet does, and this in turn creates a much softer, quicker-to-break-down texture. These cheeses have an inherently vegetal, bitter character, which is one of my absolute favourite styles.

Secondly, you will find vegetal flavours appearing in cheeses made with traditional rennet from elsewhere in the world and typically in those with drier rinds and firmer textures. One of my favourites is a cheese called St James, made in Cumbria in England, and another called Gubbeen, from Ireland, shows these nuances well too.

Washed Rind

ORIGIN: Arrábida mountains, Portugal

FLAVOUR NOTES: Vegetal, spicy, animal

PAIRS WELL WITH: A dry white wine from Portugal like Adega de Pegões 'Selected Harvest', an IPA, or a white/rosé vermouth (like Lustau Vermut Rosé) and soda

Azeitão DOP

(Unpasteurised, Ewes' Milk, Vegetarian Coagulant)

I love visiting farmers' markets and finding a grandma in the village who is selling her cheese, which has no name. This is one reason I love to travel, to eat my way around foods and 'in particular' cheeses you cannot find outside of their production area. Although there aren't a huge variety of cheeses making their way out of Portugal, fortunately, there are some that do. One of these is Azeitão, a DOP cheese named after the foothills of the Arrábida mountains.

This is a soft, raw-milk cheese whose coagulation has taken place with the thistle coagulant we have discussed before (see page 71), one typically used in Portugal and Spain. The thistle-flower coagulant gives the cheese a very distinct taste, which you rarely see outside of Portugal and Spain. It gives a vegetal bitter that is the calling card of cheeses coagulated using this method. This is a vegetal and green-tasting cheese with flavours of herbs and grasses alongside a pronounced acidity, spice and animal profile.

Washed Rind

If you like Azeitão DOP, you'll also like La Retorta.

ORIGIN: Extremadura, Spain

FLAVOUR NOTES: Vegetal, artichoke, bitter

PAIRS WELL WITH: A fino or manzanilla dry sherry like
Hidalgo La Gitana Manzanilla, a wheat beer, or a lemonade like
San Pellegrino Limonata

Torta de Barros

(Unpasteurised, Ewes' Milk, Vegetarian Coagulant)

Torta de Barros is a fantastic example of one of my favourite styles of cheese, the Torta. Torta de Barros is made with ewes' milk and a thistle coagulant. As we have just read on page 71, the coagulant works slightly differently to animal rennet and other vegetarian coagulants, as it makes cheeses that are very runny in texture.

The first few of these Torta styles were an accidental discovery – cheesemakers making semi-hard cheeses would, at certain times of the year, find that their cheeses turned very creamy and runny, and so were considered faulty and given to the shepherds to eat. Eventually, they figured that the reverse proteolysis (the cheese turning to goo) was because of cooler temperatures and high humidity in the foggy winter air – an excellent discovery which is now replicated in the cheese-maturing facilities to make these textures intentionally.

As well as having a dreamy texture, this cheese, which you need to eat with a spoon, has wonderful flavours. Torta de Barros has its characteristic vegetal bitter, with notes of artichoke alongside the creamy interior. This cheese also has a savoury and farmy character from the rind-washing itself, giving an extra layer of complexity, making this my favourite Torta style.

Washed Rind

If you like Torta de Barros, you'll also like Mont D'Or AOP.

ORIGIN: Cumbria, England

FLAVOUR NOTES: Vegetal, gamey, herby

PAIRS WELL WITH: Late harvest sweet wines, fruity, botanical gins such as Boxer gin, or dark rum

St James

(Unpasteurised, Ewes' Milk, Traditional Rennet)

St James is an incredibly special cheese made by Martin Gott in Cumbria. It is made using the milk from his 250+ ewes, which are Lacaune with some crossings. Laucane is a breed known predominantly for its milk being used in Roquefort production. This cheese is made seasonally, with the peak of the production in May to June, when he is transforming 350 to 400 litres per day. This swings enormously, and by August, the yield goes down to about 100 litres a day. The tups (rams) go in on the glorious twelfth (of August) each year and, eight weeks from then, the flock will be dry and the production of cheese stops for the season.

Martin doesn't use commercial starter cultures (see glossary), which means that he doesn't buy his cultures pre-made. He makes his own farm-origin cultures at the start of each season using raw milk from his herd on his farm. This gives the cheese its originality and a real sense of place.

I first met Martin several years back when he came to visit the shop I was working in. We were destined to get on as we started talking about pairings and I brought out a bottle of Boxer gin to try with the cheese, which was a very tasty match.

St James, while having certain signature flavour profiles, does not always appear in the same guise. Flavours vary wildly from batch to batch and even wheel to wheel (or square to square, as it is made in this shape). The texture can be dense and slightly feathered at the core and in some batches the paste is soft and completely broken down. In flavour, St James can be vegetal, meaty, gamey, brothy and beyond.

Washed Rind

If you like St James, you may also like Taleggio DOP.

ORIGIN: Ceredigion, Wales

FLAVOUR NOTES: Vegetal, meaty, buttery

PAIRS WELL WITH: A Rutherglen Muscat like Campbells
Rutherglen Muscat, a VSOP Calvados, or
an oak-aged medium-sweet cider

Celtic Promise

(Unpasteurised, Cows' Milk, Traditional Rennet)

I first tried Celtic Promise back around 2012 when I was working in the cheese room at Whole Foods Market. I put together a washed-rind display for autumn, and this stinker caught my attention. As well as enjoying the flavour profile, I loved it as a monger because it was one of the easiest washed-rind cheeses to cut, serve and display. This is also a feature to bear in mind when choosing your cheeses for a cheeseboard – runny cheeses are beautiful, but highly impractical if you need to portion them.

Celtic Promise is made on Glynhynod Farm in the west of Wales. It is a Caerphilly recipe which has been washed in brine to evolve into something new. It is made at the oldest artisan cheese dairy in Wales by a team that I have been fortunate to meet on several occasions over recent years. Robert, who is now in charge of running the business, has continued his parents' vision of using the best raw milk and natural methods, which is apparent in both the company's ethos and the flavour of the cheeses.

Celtic Promise is wonderfully vegetal, herby and savoury. It is complex and, even within the same wheel, I have tasted Marmite, Bovril, Brussels sprouts, peach, rich beefy notes, gravy and butter. Its texture is more giving than a Caerphilly, due to its wash, and this is a cheese that lends itself very well to cooking also. Melt it over potatoes and the job's a good 'un.

Washed Rind

If you like Celtic Promise, you'll also like Maroilles.

ORIGIN: West Cork, Ireland

FLAVOUR NOTES: Vegetal, brothy, nutty

PAIRS WELL WITH: An Amontillado sherry, an Irish whiskey, or a Guinness Extra Stout

Gubbeen

(Pasteurised, Cows' Milk, Traditional Rennet)

Gubbeen is a cheese made by the Ferguson family, on a 250-acre farm in West Cork. The farm is on the coast, one mile away from the fishing village of Schull. This idyllic area not only boasts some fantastic scenery, but with Mount Gabriel to the north, the herd and the farm are also well sheltered and protected. This spot is where the Gulf Stream regularly comes in, so the warmer weather actually allows for earlier grass growth and the herd being put out on pasture earlier, aspects that are integral to the quality and flavour profiles found in the cheese.

Gubbeen is washed in a brine solution with the addition of a touch of white wine. The cheese has a beautiful rose pink and white hue to it. It is very distinctive. Analyses have led to the discovery that this pinkish white microorganism is, in fact, native to Gubbeen farm and has thus been named *Microbacterium gubbeenense*.

I adore its texture. It is chubby and pliable with a good spring back when you give it a pudge (squeeze). Gubbeen boasts flavours from the land. Think mushroom, forest and vegetal notes. It also makes a mean toastie.

Washed Rind

If you like Gubbeen, you may also like Saint-Nectaire AOP.

FLAVOUR
FRUIT

Fruity is a flavour descriptor we use a lot for both food and wine. Although it's universally understood, 'fruity' doesn't really mean anything on its own. We can imagine it as a feeling, meaning being jovial or spritely, or in flavour, it can generally mean bright, fresh or sweet. But 'fruity' really needs context to know what flavours are showing. As a red wine may have blackcurrant and blackberry notes, a fruity cheese will have the same specificity if you think hard enough. We see fruity flavours in washed rinds as well as hard cheeses (like pineapple in Lincolnshire Poacher) and blues (such as pears in Montagnolo Affine), but here, we are looking at fruity flavours in washed-rind cheeses specifically.

Fruit flavours can come through in multiple ways. As we have learned, washed-rind cheeses can be doused in a mixture of a brine solution plus an alcohol and this imparts flavour. In this section, we will see the aptly named Stinking Bishop. It is a real stinker; however, its palate is softer and gentler. The cheese is washed in a pear brandy, and this imparts some flavour onto the cheese. Fruit flavours can appear even if they are not part of the wash, such as the unmistakeable peachy notes which come through in Mahón DOP (page 78). The cheese hasn't been near a peach, just as a wine hasn't been near a blackcurrant; these are just chemical compounds that are released during the life of a cheese. Fruit can even be added into the cheese, as in Wensleydale with cranberries or a Basajo with fruit atop, and in these instances, the fruit flavour is real, and hopefully easy to identify.

ORIGIN: Menorca, Spain

FLAVOUR NOTES: Peachy, buttery, salty

PAIRS WELL WITH: Floral white wines like Verdejo, a dry Madeira like
H&H 10-Year-Old Sercial Madeira, or an amber ale

Mahón DOP

(Unpasteurised or Pasteurised, Cows' Milk, Traditional Rennet)

Mahón is a cheese which completely stole into my affections when I
started retailing way back when. It is an orange-rinded, square-pillow-
shaped cheese from Menorca. Back in the nineteenth century, travelling
salesmen would have visited the island selling their wares – ploughs,
equipment and suchlike. The farmers who weren't the most affluent
would purchase these items using cheese as currency. The travelling
salesmen would then store the young cheeses before selling them on,
accidentally dipping into the profession of affinage.

The orange colouring comes from a coating of olive oil and paprika.
This semi-hard cheese can be sold anywhere once it's reached two
months old. I recommend trying them at this younger age, as the rind
has an unmistakeable peach aroma to it. The rind does vary and while
you can taste peach and fruits in certain wheels (pillows?), others have a
damper, more earthy character. The paste of the cheese sits in between
a Cheddar and Gouda texture when aged a little longer. I have
discovered that the very young, straight-out-the-mould cheeses are also
sold locally and are particularly delicious, fresh and zingy, which I cannot
wait to seek out. To Menorca!

Washed Rind

If you like Mahón DOP, you'll also like Gubbeen.

ORIGIN: Northern Italy

FLAVOUR NOTES: Stone fruit, yeasty, meaty

PAIRS WELL WITH: A fruity red wine like a Negroamaro, a Belgian Tripel beer, or a Negroni

Taleggio DOP

(Unpasteurised and Pasteurised, Cows' Milk, Traditional Rennet)

Taleggio is the first cheese I completely fell in lust with. While others have been cheese flings, this is a long-lasting love affair. Taleggio is a washed-rind cheese from Italy with an orange rind and a chubby-baby texture. There is a French phrase that you use when you squidge a baby's cheek, 'Je veux te manger', and this is exactly what I want to do to these cheeses – squidge their face AND eat them. When ripe, it has a beautiful bulge and a custardy texture that I could eat forever. Taleggio is made with both pasteurised or raw milk and, although the pasteurised milk version is sessionable and fruity, the raw-milk versions, especially the one matured by casArrigoni, are on another level. The milk comes from several small farms in the Valley of Taleggio (Val Taleggio).

Taleggio has a punchy aroma which boasts more volume than its flavour. There is an incredibly fruity, yogurty and slightly sour profile that I adore in Taleggio, rounded off with a vegetal outer. It is a fabulous melting cheese. Try the combination of 'nduja and Taleggio in a toastie, on a pizza, in a burger or any other melted recipe for a fabulous food explosion.

Washed Rind

If you like Taleggio DOP, you'll also like Mont D'Or AOP.

ORIGIN: Franche-Comté, France

FLAVOUR NOTES: Fruity, yogurty, resinous

PAIRS WELL WITH: a sparkling rosé like
Bolney Cuvée Rosé, or pu-erh tea

Mont D'Or AOP

(Unpasteurised, Cows' Milk, Traditional Rennet)

The one thing that keeps me from going into a full post-summer slump when the days start getting shorter is the bustle of excitement around the arrival of Mont D'Or. Its production in France starts on 15 August each year, and it is then about a month's countdown until the arrival of one of my favourite cheeses onto our counters. There is absolutely no time to be sad that the summer is over when Mont D'Or is on its way. (That sadness can be saved for February, the worst month in the calendar.)

Mont D'Or (aka Vacherin du Haut-Doubs, aka Vacherin) is a cheese commonly associated with Christmas, even if the first cheeses of the season are available from mid-September.

Mont D'Or is a soft cheese from the same region as Comté. It is traditionally made in the aforementioned timeline, as the cows come down from the mountains and off pasture. As the animals head into the latter part of their lactation cycle, their milk yields drop, resulting in a higher fat content that is much better suited to soft cheesemaking instead of the large, hard wheels of Comté. Even though the production of Mont D'Or has developed from farmhouse into larger production, it has remained a seasonal cheese.

It is supple, with stone fruit flavours and a crème-fraîche acidity in its youth. As it ages, it becomes more animal, sprucey and punchy in its flavours. It makes a fabulous melter, and as it comes in its own wooden box (it would run all over the place if not), is the perfect self-contained fondue.

Washed Rind

If you like Mont D'Or AOP, you'll also like Rush Creek Reserve.

ORIGIN: Franche-Comté, France

FLAVOUR NOTES: Fruity, yogurty, buttery

PAIRS WELL WITH: A Pinot Noir like Thibault
Liger-Belair Nuits-Saint-Georges 'La Charmotte',
or a fruity whisky like Glenmorangie Original

Morbier AOP

(Unpasteurised, Cows' Milk, Traditional Rennet)

Morbier is not a blue cheese. That's a good place to start. If I had a pound for every time that I offered this to a customer and they replied, 'I don't like blue cheese', I would have several more pounds than the collection in my Brillat-Savarin piggy bank. Morbier is a cheese from the same region as Comté. It is a chubby-baby style of cheese, which has a bounce-back texture and almost sticky paste.

This cheese could sit in two style categories – it is a semi-hard cheese in texture – however, I have chosen to group it based on its washed-rind element.

Morbier is a great melting cheese and can be used in place of Raclette, if you are unable to source it – or simply to make a different dish. A few colleagues and I made a 'Morbiflette' (our take on Raclette) and 'Morbi-chips' for staff lunch once, and I can vouch for these being most delicious.

It is a shy cheese and really needs to be brought up to room temperature to taste the subtle nuances. You will then find fruit, yogurt, butter and even a fudgy sweetness coming through, making this an incredibly moreish cheese. I recommend eating the rind on most cheeses, and especially this one, to give an extra dimension to its earthy exterior.

Washed Rind

If you like Morbier AOP, you'll also like Raclette.

ORIGIN: Gloucestershire, England

FLAVOUR NOTES: Fruity, buttery, sweet

PAIRS WELL WITH: A Canadian ice cider, a Vieille Prune (Plum)
eau de vie, or a sparkling soft drink like Belvoir
Botanical Juniper & Tonic

Stinking Bishop

(Pasteurised, Cows' Milk, Vegetarian Coagulant)

Stinking Bishop is a cheese with a bark much worse than its bite. I have opened one in confined spaces several times and, even as a seasoned cheesemonger, it does wake you up and tickle the nostrils.

Cheese has been made at Hunts Court in Gloucestershire since the 1970s, when Charles Martell hand-milked his three Old Gloucester cows. The first cheese produced was a Double Gloucester, and Stinking Bishop followed a while after, in 1994.

Stinking Bishop really does have some incredibly pungent aromas owing to the process of washing its rind. However, its name does not come from this stench. Stinking Bishop is the name of one of the varieties of pear, which is transformed into perry, the alcohol used to wash the cheese. The resulting aromas are full and quite bodily, but the flavour itself is sweet, fruity, buttery and surprisingly mellow. It is a cheese whose rind odours really do stay on you, so it is one that I wouldn't recommend eating like an apple. Unless you have gloves.

Washed Rind

If you like Stinking Bishop, you'll also like Taleggio DOP.

FLAVOUR
SAVOURY

I have a sweet tooth. I adore sugary drinks and I have a separate compartment in my stomach for dessert. No matter how much I have eaten before, there is always room for something chocolatey, or ice cream or sorbet. Fortunately, my body tells me when enough is enough, and if I am ever in a situation where I have eaten too much of something sweet, it then tells me to stop and starts craving something savoury. When I crave something savoury or when my body is telling me to switch gear to get off the sweet highway, I am generally craving crisps or steak. But mostly crisps. I love crisps.

Savoury flavours in cheese are reminiscent of other foodstuffs, which generally have been cooked. Therefore, in savoury cheeses you find flavours of meat, roasted vegetables, gravy and even Marmite and Bovril. Savoury is generally associated with strong flavours and salt, as you can see, and we are now working into the big, bold statement flavours of washed-rind cheeses. The savoury element in cheese is bold, rounded and complex. Yeasty is a flavour which comes through time and time again with washed-rind cheeses such as Époisses (page 84), and you will see it later in the Blue chapter, with cheeses such as Stichelton (page 166), which exhibits a washed-rind characteristic on its rind.

Époisses AOP

(Unpasteurised or Pasteurised, Cows' Milk, Traditional Rennet)

This is the cheese with three silent 's's, according to some ('Oh, I love Epwah!'), and the protagonist in myths about not being able to carry it on public transport in France. Époisses (actually pronounced 'Eh-pwass') is a cheese with a full aroma and a powerful but accessible flavour. Its pungent smell could knock over a small child or middle-sized adult; this is a cheese you KNOW is in your fridge. This is also an excellent fridge cheese for a house share with folks you are perhaps not so fond of.

Its aroma is of Marmite, gravy, cooked brassica and nuts. On the palate, this delicious, custardy mess is fruity, sweet and with a savoury, yeasty and vegetal flavour profile. I'm always pleasantly surprised at how rounded the flavours are after smelling such a statement perfume. If you fancy an extravagant baking cheese, I was told by a restaurateur that it works beautifully with crème de cassis. I brought some to work a few years ago, but I never got around to trying the combination. If anyone tries it, let me know!

Washed Rind

If you like Époisses AOP, you will also like Edmund Tew.

ORIGIN: Pays de Herve, Belgium

FLAVOUR NOTES: Savoury, yeasty, buttery

PAIRS WELL WITH: An aromatic white wine like a Gewumlautrztraminer, or a peaty whisky like Ardbeg 10 Year Old

Fromage de Herve AOP

(Pasteurised, Cows' Milk, Traditional Rennet)

Fromage de Herve is the only Belgian cheese with an Appelation d'Origine Protegée (AOP). It is a cheese with a long history, dating back to the thirteenth century. However, its expansion really occurred in the sixteenth century, when Charles V forbade the export of cereal to the Netherlands. This law forced farmers to stop growing grain, as they were no longer able to valorise it through export. Instead, they shifted into a different sector of agriculture, breeding dairy cows for milk. With the desire to valorise this milk and to transform it into a product with a much longer shelf life, they moved into cheesemaking, expanding on the existing numbers and production of Fromage de Herve cheese.

As well as being eaten, as you would expect with a cheese, it was used as currency and rent, and a by-product was made from it named Remoudou – a second milking of the cows to trick the tax man (you will see this more with Reblochon, page 90). It is a small, cube-shaped cheese with a heady aroma. Its paste is pliable and flavours are yeasty, savoury and buttery. Its characteristic orange colour comes from the bacteria which are encouraged in the washing process, and not by any additional colouring, which is not permitted by the AOP.

Washed Rind

If you like Fromage de Herve AOP, you'll also like Maroilles.

ORIGIN: Wisconsin, USA

FLAVOUR NOTES: Savoury, brothy, sweet

PAIRS WELL WITH: A sparkling wine like Louis Roederer Quartet, Speyside whisky, or smoked Märzen lager like Schlenkerla

Rush Creek Reserve

(Unpasteurised, Cows' Milk, Traditional Rennet)

Now, then. A cheese which is based on the style of one of my all-time favourite cheeses sounds like a recipe for me disliking it. This is luckily not the case – it is most excellent. Rush Creek Reserve is a washed-rind, spruce-bound (wrapped in a belt of spruce wood to hold its shape and give flavour) soft cheese made in the style of a French spruce-banded cheese.

This cheese is only made in the autumn, when the cows transition their diet over from the rich pastures to their winter feed of dry hay. The founders were among some of the first people in the USA to feed their cows using a rotational grazing system seasonally, and always pasture-based. This natural system, with a concentration on the soil, feed, cows and, consequently, milk is why this cheese and its sister (from the same producer, Uplands Cheese), Pleasant Ridge Reserve, are two of the best cheeses you can find from the USA.

I have only been lucky enough to try this cheese twice in my life, but it is so special that I have very strong mental flavour memories. The cheese has a supple, crème-anglaise texture with a whole plethora of flavours coming through. It is savoury, sprucey, bacony and slightly woody, but it also has a sweetness which balances this out. To eat Rush Creek Reserve, you will generally require a spoon and not a knife. At the age profile it is sold at, the texture is fully broken down and you really want to scoop it like a yogurt. A great big savoury cheesy pudding.

Washed Rind

If you like Rush Creek Reserve, you will also like Winnimere.

ORIGIN: Kent, England

FLAVOUR NOTES: Soft, brothy, farmy

PAIRS WELL WITH: A Chardonnay like Sylvain Bzikot Puligny-Montrachet, an abbey beer, or a dry cider

Edmund Tew

(Unpasteurised, Cows' Milk, Traditional Rennet)

Edmund Tew is a small, lactic washed-rind cheese made by Australian-born David Holton in the south of England. David makes his cheeses on Bore Place, home to an organic farm, a stone's throw away from the dairy. The farm practises techniques which concentrate on the health of the soil, and both the high animal welfare and farming practices translate into excellent milk. The cheese is a newer style in the UK, having been made for just nine years.

It is easily identified by the wrinkled, brain-like appearance from its *Geotrichum* rind. *Geotrichum* is the yeast that forms on the surfaces of soft cheeses (we saw this in St Jude on page 39 and Brightwell Ash on page 38), and it is actively encouraged and enhanced in this recipe. Whereas some washed-rind cheeses in this style are washed in an alcohol like an eau de vie, Edmund Tew is washed simply in brine, allowing the nuances of the milk to come through. The cheese is handmade and matured by David, who is not only a cheesemaker but also an affineur. It is named after a convict sent to Australia for stealing cheese and is as naughty as its namesake. Its texture is moussey when young and broken down and gooey when aged. A moreish umami dominates with ramen broth, Marmite and Bovril as regular flavour contenders.

Washed Rind

If you like Edmund Tew, you'll also like St Cera.

FLAVOUR
FARMY

I love this flavour profile. I like the shock factor, and to make people question their whole palate and integrity. The word 'farmy' really does divide a room. There are some cheeses which really are so graphic in their aroma and flavour profile that they do not let you forget where they have come from. These are your farmy, barny and animal flavours and aromas. Some even border on the faecal. Yum. Washed-rind cheeses can transport you into the armpit of a cow. These cheeses really give you a sense of place. They put a cheese firmly into context, instead of providing a dissociated tasting experience and, as with most strong flavours, it is all about moderation. These flavours can come from several factors, including the yeasts and their accelerated growth owing to the washing of the cheeses. Try not to be put off by this flavour – it is very natural, as we are eating a product that has come from an animal.

Many goats' cheeses are also farmy and barnyardy, which we saw in detail in the 'Aged Fresh' section, where we learned about the volatile short-chain fatty acids. You will see a theme in this section: all the cheeses I have chosen come from France and Switzerland. They are not the only countries to make farmy cheeses, but they are certainly the flagship producers of this style.

ORIGIN: Normandy, France

FLAVOUR NOTES: Farmy, hazelnut, sweet

PAIRS WELL WITH: An aromatic white like Torrontés,
a cider from Normandy, or an Apple Margarita

Le Pont l'Évêque AOP

(Unpasteurised, Pasteurised or Thermised, Cows' Milk, Traditional Rennet)

Le Pont l'Évêque is a cheese I have been eating since I was a child. My family were huge Francophiles, so we travelled to Normandy frequently, and my grandma had French ancestors, which may partly explain my obsession with cheese. This cheese is now named after the village of Pont l'Évêque in Normandy, although it didn't take this name until the seventeenth century. Le Pont l'Évêque, Livarot and Neufchâtel cheeses all come from a common ancestor cheese named Angelot, which was mentioned by poet Guillaume de Lorris in his thirteenth-century poem 'Roman de la Rose'. The cheese itself was created by Cistercian monks.

Pont l'Évêque comes in a square format and in a nifty box to stop the pong from completely escaping – and to keep its shape. It has a very barnyardy and farmy aroma with notes of straw and earth. On the palate, as with most strongly scented cheeses, it is a little sweet, hazelnutty, sticky-textured and with a barny aftertaste. I like to bake Pont l'Évêque into a potato gratin, a recipe you see frequently around its region. Add some leeks and bacon and you have a recipe for a very full but happy stomach.

Washed Rind

If you like Le Pont l'Évêque AOP, you'll also like Livarot AOP.

ORIGIN: Haute-Savoie, France

FLAVOUR NOTES: Farmy, fruity, buttery

PAIRS WELL WITH: An alpine white wine like Domaine Lupin Frangy Roussette de Savoie, or a pear cider

Reblochon AOP

(Unpasteurised, Cows' Milk, Traditional Rennet)

This is another cheese which has a firm VIP seat on my Christmas cheeseboard each year. I love Reblochon and I want you to love it too! It is a soft, supple-textured, washed-rind cheese from the Savoie region of France. Its name comes from the verb *'reblocher'* meaning 'to pinch again', referring to the milking of the animals. Historically, the landowners, who were typically monks or nobles, effected a tax *'droit d'ociège'*, which was based on the quantity of milk produced per day. To minimise this tax, on the day that they were checked, the farmers would only milk their animals partially, to make it seem as though they had less milk. Once the landowners left, the farmers would re-milk the animals (reblocher) to retrieve the remaining milk, which was used to make Reblochon. Cheeky.

It is the cheese used in the recipe for tartiflette, where you plonk a Reblochon on top of potatoes, cream, lardons and onions and bake it into a delicious, calorific winter warmer of a meal. Reblochon lends itself well to melting, but it is also a great cheeseboard cheese. Its peachy rind gives some very funky, farmy aromas, bordering on manure at times – yes, cheese which smells like poo can be delicious. On the palate in younger cheeses, you find notes of yogurt and fruits like strawberries and grape soda. As the cheese continues to be aged on, it develops its character and enters the realms of the farm and barnyard. On paper, I understand that this may sound horrendous, but trust me and give it a go!

Washed Rind

If you like Reblochon AOP, you'll also like Mont D'Or AOP.

ORIGIN: Hauts-de-France, France

FLAVOUR NOTES: Farmy, buttery, sweet

PAIRS WELL WITH: Sweet Loire white wines, Somerset Pomona apple liqueur, or Trappist/abbey beers

Maroilles AOP

(Unpasteurised, Pasteurised or Thermised, Cows' Milk, Traditional Rennet)

Maroilles is an incredibly old recipe of a cheese, dating back to the tenth century, when it is said to have been created in the Abbey des Maroilles, which was unfortunately subsequently destroyed during the French Revolution.

This cheese absolutely stinks to high heaven. It is renowned for being one of the most pungent – and, my goodness, this is true. It is washed twice a week for several weeks and matured in very humid conditions, just like your feet in socks on a hot day. It is powerfully farmy and barnyard-like in aroma, with a sweet, farmy and rounded palate. It is hugely relevant to cuisine in its area of production in the north of France, where it is transformed into sauces, cheesecakes, macarons and, most famously, tarte au Maroilles, an emblematic dish from Normandy. It is a tart made using puff pastry or pizza dough, with lashings of crème fraîche, eggs, seasoning and Maroilles, sitting centre stage. Perhaps pair this with a salad leaf for a lighter option.

Washed Rind

If you like Maroilles AOP, you'll also like socks . . .

ORIGIN: Canton du Valais, and Kandersteg, Switzerland

FLAVOUR NOTES: Sweet, creamy, nutty

PAIRS WELL WITH: A light red wine like Zweigelt,
an IPA, or a Dirty Martini with pickle juice

Raclette du Valais AOP

(Unpasteurised, Cows' Milk, Traditional Rennet)

Just looking at the word 'Raclette' conjures up cosy wintertime images for me, with melted cheese, cornichons, woollen jumpers and roaring fires. However, in the Valaisian style, it is eaten in summer, scraped from half a wheel of cheese.

The name comes from the verb *'racler'*, meaning to scrape, which thank goodness sounds miles sexier in French than in English. When the cheese is heated in preparation for pouring it over potatoes, it is scraped off the rest of the cheese and onto a plate. Raclette was not always called Raclette. Melting cheeses of this style have been around in the Valais since the sixteenth century. However, the name 'Raclette' only came about in the late nineteenth century.

Raclette du Valais is made exclusively in the Swiss Canton of Valais, and in Kandersteg, in the Canton of Bern. One of the breeds of cow whose milk is used for its production is the Hérens/Eringer. These ladies form a natural herd hierarchy, with one cow becoming the 'queen'. This has been exploited somewhat in Valais, where 'le Combat des Reines' is an organised fight of sorts, but a jovial one, where the cows' horns are blunted and they push each other around a little bit.

Like many of these washed-rind cheeses, it has a very powerful odour, reminiscent of gym changing rooms and bad breath. You must get past these and get into the taste. The flavours are farmy yet sweet, buttery and rich.

Washed Rind

If you like Raclette du Valais AOP, you'll also like Ashcombe.

Munster AOP

(Unpasteurised, Pasteurised or Thermised, Cows' Milk, Traditional Rennet)

Munster is another cheese that stinks. My goodness. I have trauma from going home after Christmas cheesemonger shifts smelling of the stuff after having accidentally glanced at a Munster. This and Roquefort are VERY clingy. They like to stay with you.

It is a washed-rind cheese from the region of Alsace. Its name derives from 'monastery' (in French *'monastère'*) as it was first created by monks in the seventh century. The area sees a lot of rain, which promotes the growth of lush pastures that, feed the cows whose milk is used to make the cheese. You will sometimes see Munster with cumin, as meadow cumin (*cumin des prés*) is a plant commonly found in the Vosges.

Munster and Maroilles are two of the punchiest washed-rind cheeses I have ever encountered. There is no doubt when they are on the counter or in your fridge. Munster has a hugely concentrated flavour with a rich umami and farmy flavour, and a sweetness preventing it from getting too animal. If you are feeling really brave, you can try a Munster sauce on a steak or *jambonneau* (the knuckle end of a pork leg or ham) in the region. I did this in mid-July in Alsace and instantly regretted it. When in Rome . . . but perhaps not Rome in the middle of a heatwave.

Washed Rind

If you like Munster AOP, you'll also like Maroilles AOP.

Semi-Hard

Four

The enjoyment of eating cheese is not just about the wonderful array of flavours we find. In the Fresh chapter we saw that cheeses such as Mozzarella di Bufala have very subtle, simple flavours, but we still adore them. The texture of a cheese is hugely important in our overall perception and enjoyment, and this chapter is the one which illustrates this to me the most.

This chapter may, from its name, seem like a bit of a dumping ground for anything which doesn't fit perfectly into a hard or a soft category, but I have broken this down into two distinct textural styles.

Firstly, we have Tomme-style cheeses, which have a bit of a squidge to them and many of which can be very good at melting. These include a selection of my favourite 'chubby babies' (my term for cheeses whose cheeks you want to squeeze) and session cheeses (again not a technical name, but my term for any cheese I can eat continuously without being overwhelmed by complexity or intensity of flavour). Because I've worked for a French company for a long time – in addition to enjoying many a visit across the Channel – I have an enormous soft spot for this Tomme-style cheese. The most famous type is named Tomme de Savoie (page 100), which you will learn more about in this chapter. These cheeses are around the 1 to 2kg mark, and many have a characteristic grey/brown rind. Tomme de Savoie and friends are cheeses which were, and sometimes still are, made alongside another cheese. Beaufort, which features in the Hard chapter, is a cheese also made in the Savoie. It is a large wheel – I've lifted some over the 40kg threshold – and it takes a long time to mature. While maturing, the cheesemakers need sustenance – and to make a living. So these smaller cheeses named 'Tommes' were the answer.

The second style is 'crumbly'. Crumblies are a very British style of cheese, including some fantastic classics. Unlike Cheddar, which sits in the hard category, there are many British Territorials (cheeses named after their place of production) called crumblies that originate in the north of England and in Wales. You may hear the name 'Dale style' for cheeses like Wensleydale. These are characteristically crumbly in texture owing to their production techniques and slow drainage time. These cheeses are embodied by a dominant lemon acidity, minerality, freshness and tang.

FLAVOUR
EARTH

Sticking to the theme of flavours which you may not think to immediately put in your mouth, we have moved on from 'farmy' in the Washed Rind chapter and into 'earth'. There are many different flavours that can be subcategorised here. The cheeses I have chosen have a strong aroma and a gentle flavour of cave, and damp vegetation. For example, a Saint-Nectaire (page 99) is not a Saint-Nectaire if you cannot smell cave, damp straw and a bit of mud thrown in for good measure. These are flavours you can also find towards the rinds of cave-aged Cheddars and semi-hard British cheeses and, as the rind is an integral part of the cheeses in Saint-Nectaire and Tomme de Savoie, it too is an integral part of the aroma and palate. The moulds on these cheeses love damp conditions – and for this reason, they may pop up in other cheeses if moisture levels are not kept under control. In that case, they are not desirable.

Earthiness as a flavour profile is very much topical. These earthy, musty and antique-bookshop aromas and smells are prominent on rinds, but not so much in the paste as you work your way inside a cheese. Microbes native to cellars, caves and damp and humid environments will start to live on these cheese rinds and then begin to impart their cavey goodness through the production of aroma compounds.

ORIGIN: Auvergne, France

FLAVOUR NOTES: Earthy, grassy, yogurty

PAIRS WELL WITH: Gamay red wines like Côte Roannaise, a White Negroni, or a semi-dry cider like Sassy Organic Cidre

Saint-Nectaire AOP

(Unpasteurised and Pasteurised Cows' Milk, Traditional Rennet)

I have fond memories of walking round a market in Provence a few years back. It was about 10am and I had not eaten breakfast – a huge error on my part, as the exploding produce stalls were enough to whet the appetite of even the strictest non-breakfast eater. Being surrounded by temptation meant I needed a snack to get me through to lunchtime, and so I bought a substantial wedge of Saint-Nectaire and proceeded to eat it like an apple in front of the cheesemaker and around the market.

Saint-Nectaire is a cheese which may appear unappetising, with its grey and brown rind. These moulds (called mucor) are deterred in much other cheesemaking but encouraged in this recipe. The moulds are patted down and kept under control, adding to the unique flavour. Its aromas are unmistakeably earthy, cave-like, damp and on occasion, antique bookshop or Grandma's attic. On the palate, it has the most beautiful mix of a yogurt paste and buttery notes if you eat it rindless. If you eat the rind (which I highly recommend), some of the aromas you find on the nose come through on the palate. Its texture is chubby, pliable and giving. This is by far my favourite session cheese of them all.

Semi-Hard

If you like Saint-Nectaire AOP, you'll also like Tomme de Savoie AOP.

ORIGIN: Savoie, France

FLAVOUR NOTES: Earthy, fruity, mushroom

PAIRS WELL WITH: A medium-bodied rosé like Château Ksara Sunset Rosé, or a pale ale

Tomme de Savoie AOP

(Unpasteurised or Pasteurised, Cows' Milk, Traditional Rennet)

Speaking of my favourite session cheeses, meet Tomme de Savoie. Tomme de Savoie is a simple but perfect cheese. It is one which sometimes falls through the cracks for those coming in to buy their 'hard, soft and blue' combination in cheese shops, but it is one I always mention as an additional cheese if this is the case.

Tomme de Savoie is an old recipe with humble beginnings. It is a recipe which began its life as a kitchen staple and not a cheese for widespread production. In the harsh winter months in the Savoie, families would be stuck in their houses for the season, with their animals indoors close by. They would skim the limited milk from their animals to make butter and cream and the resulting skimmed milk would be turned into cheeses like Tomme de Savoie. This would serve as a delicious source of protein. Some ageing of the cheese meant it would keep long enough to get them through to the calmer spring conditions.

It is a very simple cheese. It doesn't have a huge, in-your-face character like Roquefort, Gruyère or Camembert. It is subtle and beautiful. It's a true aficionado's cheese, especially once you realise that these subtleties are, in fact, even harder to perfect, and there is nothing for the cheese to hide behind. Tomme de Savoie has a grey rind, and, like Saint-Nectaire, some choose to eat it and some choose to discard it. It is a cheese which has fruity yogurt flavours in its tacky, springy paste. I frequently taste strawberry milkshake and strawberry yogurt in this cheese, as well as it tasting strangely like a cheese sandwich (with butter included). The rind gives it an extra dimension and texture, adding earthy and cavey flavours.

Semi-Hard

If you like Tomme de Savoie AOP, you'll also like Moreton.

ORIGIN: West Cork, Ireland

FLAVOUR NOTES: Earthy, lactic, buttery

PAIRS WELL WITH: A lighter whiskey like Bushmills 10-year-old single malt, or a low-alcohol beer like Lucky Saint Unfiltered Lager

Carraignamuc

(Unpasteurised, Cows' Milk, Traditional Rennet)

Mike Parle and Darcie Mayland, who make Carraignamuc, only started making cheese in 2020. Their aim was to make a cheese in the same style as they work their land, with minimal intervention and to be as true to that terroir as possible. This cheese is made with the milk from just five cows. Their cows are autochthonous, or indigenous, breeds (Droimeann and Irish Shorthorn, which are native to the area) and the starter cultures they use are farm-made, using their own milk.

The cheese is loosely based around a cheese called Macagn, produced in the mountains of the Biellese Alps and Valsesia in Italy. Their cheese came about from discussions between Mike, Darcie, and Max Jones, a good friend of mine and fellow cheesemonger turned food conservationist.

This is the reinvention of a true native farmhouse Irish cheese, using the native flora in the milk to create a sense of place. Carraignamuc is a lactic, slightly crumbly cheese with a little breakdown just beneath the rind. The flavours are earthy and buttery, yet with a zippy acidity and lactic tang.

Semi-Hard

If you like Carraignamuc, you'll also like Macagn.

ORIGIN: Suffolk, England

FLAVOUR NOTES: Earthy, grassy, yogurty

PAIRS WELL WITH: A Savagnin or Chardonnay from the Jura,
a Tawny Port Old Fashioned, or matcha tea

St Helena

(Unpasteurised, Cows' Milk, Traditional Rennet)

St Helena is a very new cheese made in Suffolk. Blake Bowden – the brain and hands behind it – has created this semi-hard and unpasteurised cheese. Blake works with Julie Cheyney at Fen Farm making St Jude (page 39) and is a talented cheesemaker. Within the last few years, he has started to develop his own products there. I have tasted numerous trials and versions of this cheese, all with enormous potential. However, the batch I tasted in summer 2021 was exceptional and I knew then that it had come into its own.

St Helena uses Montbéliarde milk from Fen Farm, the same milk which makes St Jude and Baron Bigod (pages 39 and 49). Blake makes this cheese twice a week and it is a much quicker make than the St Jude, so they are able to make the cheeses alongside each other without the dairy descending into chaos.

St Helena, like Saint-Nectaire (page 99), is a cheese whose rind is integral to the aroma and flavour profile. Characteristically matured in humid conditions, the rinds develop an earthy, cavey flavour. In addition, this cheese is rich, buttery, smooth, grassy and yeasty.

Semi-Hard

If you like St Helena, you'll also like Saint-Nectaire AOP.

ORIGIN: Vermont, Pennsylvania, and & Connecticut, USA

FLAVOUR NOTES: Earthy, fruity, grassy

PAIRS WELL WITH: A fruity red such as a Monastrell, or a Best Bitter beer

Cornerstone

(Unpasteurised, Cows' Milk, Traditional Rennet)

I could not write this book spanning different styles and types of make around the world and not include Cornerstone. For a book that is based on the premise of flavour, this cheese is not the most intuitive choice on my part, but it is incredibly special and must take pride of place.

This is a true new American classic, a cheese which is its own entity and not an imitation of another. Cornerstone is a cheese whose recipe does not belong to just one cheesemaker.

Spearheaded by Parish Hill Creamery, this is a cheese that came to being as a concept, a project, and an idea of expressing cultures, terroir and natural cheesemaking. Cornerstone is made by not one but three different creameries. Parish Hill Creamery in Vermont, Birch Run Hills Farm in Pennsylvania, and Cato Corner Farm in Connecticut. The cheese is an expression of the raw milk from these different places, their native cultures, their animals and, although the base recipe is the same, the cheeses all present the diversity of these parameters differently.

Cornerstone is a semi-hard cheese whose flavour is hard to categorise, and the more you learn about it, the more you realise that this is its intention. Owing to its natural rind, earthy flavours are common to all three iterations of this cheese, but as you would expect, the flavours in these cheeses are hard to pin down, owing to the raw milk, native cultures and natural rind.

Semi-Hard

If you like Cornerstone, you should make sure to try it from all three producers

You will notice here that the cheeses are all British except one. This is a very particular style of cheese which appears predominantly in the north of England and in Wales. These are known as 'crumbly' cheeses, and they are characterised by a crumbly texture and a higher acidity than other British cheeses like Cheddar. These characteristics come from the way the cheeses are made, with a slower drainage (of whey from the curds) than a Cheddar and so the cheese 'decalcifies'. Think about brittle bones – with less calcium, our bones aren't as strong. With less calcium in the cheese, it crumbles and fall apart, not holding together like a Cheddar. The acidity in these cheeses is very pronounced. It is lemony and mouthwatering. When you feel your saliva glands starting to go, this is the detection of acidity. As with wine, you can identify acidity by tilting your head forward to physically feel the saliva coming towards the front of your mouth (but be careful you don't dribble on your feet). The main characteristics of these cheeses are milky and fresh notes and zesty, clean and lemony flavours. These are a style of cheese that I crave and missed when I worked at Mons, who specialise in French cheeses, as this style really is typical to the UK.

Semi-Hard

ORIGIN: Northern England, UK

FLAVOUR NOTES: Lemon, mineral, tangy

PAIRS WELL WITH: A medium-bodied red wine like Carignan, an amber ale like Fuller's London Pride, or a medium-dry cider

Cheshire

(Unpasteurised and Pasteurised, Cows' Milk, Traditional and Vegetarian Coagulant)

Cheshire is an acid, crumbly cheese from the north-west of England. Once made by every farm in Cheshire, most producers of Cheshire cheese are now creameries, with just a handful of farmhouse cheesemakers – and only one of those uses raw milk. In 1914 there were over 2,000 farms making unpasteurised, traditional, clothbound Cheshire. However, the milk marketing board regulations (set up in 1933) triggered a vast decline in this farmhouse production.

The sole remaining farmhouse raw-milk producer is named Appleby's Cheshire. Sarah and Paul Appleby make a clothbound truckle, their flagship cheese whose curds use an addition of annatto, a natural food colouring (plant derivative) that gives a peach/orange hue to the cheese. For the purist, they also make a Cheshire cheese which has not been coloured.

This traditional recipe differs enormously from creamery Cheshire. For starters it is not made in a block, but in a truckle, and it is clothbound. It uses traditional starters and undergoes a long acidic maturation, and this all contributes to its organoleptic characteristics.

The creamery cheeses have a firm yet crumbly texture, moisture still within the paste and a citrusy, high acidity. They are bright white in colour and make your mouth water and pucker.

The Cheshire from Appleby's is mineral, lemony and more rounded than the creamery Cheshire. I was given an excellent, if a little leftfield, tasting of Cheshire a few years back at a hospitality festival called PX+. A London butcher made me an 'amuse bouche' using a small piece of firepit-toasted bread, steak and melted Appleby's Cheshire rind. What a delicious way to avoid waste!

Semi-Hard

If you like Cheshire, you'll also like Wensleydale.

ORIGIN: Yorkshire, England

FLAVOUR NOTES: Acid, lemon, tang

PAIRS WELL WITH: Malmsey Madeira, English strong ale, or rhubarb and apple juice

Yorkshire Wensleydale PGI

(Unpasteurised and Pasteurised, Cows' Milk, Traditional Rennet and Vegetarian Coagulant)

Like Cheshire (page 105), Yorkshire Wensleydale is a British crumbly cheese. Wensleydale was originally a sheeps'-milk cheese made in monasteries. It also used to be a blue cheese! When the country moved towards cow dairy farming in the seventeenth century, the recipe evolved into one made using cows' milk. Wensleydale, however, is now made mainly by creameries. Recently, there have been some exciting additions to the industry, with new-age cheesemakers starting to recreate the older, traditional recipe. These more traditional recipes are cheeses with a higher moisture content, less crumble and less acidity. One of these, named Old Roan (page 108), you will see later in the chapter.

Yorkshire Wensleydale has a lemon zest feel to it and a milky, mineral and almost honeyed sweetness. Aside from the traditional Yorkshire Wensleydale, a whole array of flavour variations has been developed. Wensleydale with cranberries is by far the most popular and widespread, which is funny, as I hardly see a cranberry in a UK supermarket or fruit and vegetable shop. To obtain this fruity version, Wensleydale cheeses are formed, then broken up into pieces, mixed with fruits, and re-formed before passing through an extruder. The resulting cheese is moister in texture and, with added sugar from the berries, the cheese itself is sweet and dessert-like.

Semi-Hard

106

If you like Wensleydale PGI, you will also like Cheshire.

ORIGIN: Wales and England

FLAVOUR NOTES: Acid, lemon, earthy

PAIRS WELL WITH: Dry and light white wines like Pieropan Soave Classico, or a classic pale ale like Timothy Taylor Landlord

Caerphilly

(Unpasteurised or Pasteurised, Cows' Milk,
Traditional Rennet or Vegetarian Coagulant)

Caerphilly is widely considered a Welsh cheese, as the name would suggest. It has, however, also been made in Somerset since the late nineteenth century where Cheddar makers would make it alongside their Cheddar as a way of getting cashflow before the Cheddars had matured.

Traditionally made Caerphilly originated in Wales and was a popular cheese with miners who would take some pocket cheese with them down into the pits. However, it largely died out during the Second World War as lower moisture cheeses like Cheddar were more popular because they were less perishable. By the 1950s, only one farm was still producing an authentic recipe – Duckett's in Wedmore, Somerset. Chris Duckett kept the recipe going strong and, before his passing, he moved to Westcombe Farm (who make Westcombe Cheddar) and passed on his know-how to the Carver family at Westcombe Dairy (who continue to make Duckett's Caerphilly to this day) and also to Todd Trethowan who makes Gorwydd Caerphilly.

In early 2023, new cheesemakers called the Cwmni caws Caerffili (Caerphilly Cheese Company) announced that they will be making farmhouse Caerphilly in Caerphilly, Wales for the first time in nearly 30 years.

The factory versions are very uniform in texture with small holes, an ivory paste and a slightly dry, acid crumble to the paste. It is a rindless cheese and the flavour is acidic and lemony. Farmhouse versions such as Duckett's and Gorwydd are a whole different beast. They have a rind to start. Their rinds are grey and smooth, like a Tomme de Savoie (page 100), and their pastes are not the same throughout. They have a distinction between the paste breaking down under the rind with a bit of give and a crumblier, firmer heart. Flavours are yogurt, earthy, mineral, buttery and rounded.

Semi-Hard

If you like Caerphilly, you'll also like Wensleydale.

Old Roan (Yoredale Wensleydale)

(Unpasteurised, Cows' Milk, Traditional Rennet)

Old Roan is a type of Wensleydale cheese. The Wensleydale that we know and see on cheese counters across the globe is predominantly made in large factories. Yorkshire Wensleydale used to be made in a farmstead manner until the last farmer producing it using this traditional method in the Yorkshire Dales ceased production in 1957. Since then, the cheese has only been made industrially. Old Roan, made by Ben and Sam Spence, is a revival of this traditional recipe, and it is one of the newest cheeses in this book. Ben and Sam diversified from farming into cheesemaking in 2019.

As Old Roan is made using traditional methods, instead of being produced in a factory where speed is of the essence, leading to very dry and acidic cheeses, its texture and flavour are very different. The recipe is reminiscent of how Wensleydale was made pre-World War I. It is made slower and therefore it retains more moisture and less crumble. It has a mouthwatering acidity, moreish minerality and zesty citrus notes. It is available from a select number of cheese shops only, as they are truly a micro-dairy (6m x 3m space in their converted garage!) but it is certainly one to look out for.

Semi-Hard

If you like Old Roan, you'll also like Lancashire.

ORIGIN: Brandenburg, Germany

FLAVOUR NOTES: Zesty, lemony, mineral

PAIRS WELL WITH: A golden ale such as St Peters, or a medium-dry cider

Urstromshire

(Unpasteurised, Cows' Milk, Traditional Rennet)

There is always one that breaks the mould, and in this case it goes by the name of Urstromshire, which, although it sits in this northern British, acid-cheese section, is made in Germany.

Urstromshire is a very new cheese, which was born to Paul Thomas and Yule Seifert a mere couple of years back. Paul is a British dairy technologist, and Yule a Belgian engineering-graduate-cum-cheese-specialist, and together they set up their cheesemaking business in Brandenburg, 70km south of Berlin.

With an extensive background in dairy technology, cheesemaking and retailing, the cheese power couple have created a dairy that makes a slightly eye-watering amount of cheeses. Their cheeses are mainly hybrids, owing to their understanding of and skill within cheesemaking. They have set out to pull together their desired cheesemaking techniques and flavour outcomes to make their own style of cheeses.

Urstromshire is just one of many which they make using Jersey milk. It is a clothbound cheese. The flavour is buttery, caramel just beneath the rind and with a clean acidity, its recipe not dissimilar to a Lancashire or Cheshire.

Semi-Hard

If you like Urstromshire, you'll also like Cheshire.

ORIGIN: Fife, Scotland

FLAVOUR NOTES: Yogurt, milk, tang

PAIRS WELL WITH: An unoaked Chenin Blanc, or a Nigori Saké

Anster

(Unpasteurised, Cows' Milk, Traditional Rennet)

I first tried Anster back when I was working at a grocery store, and I ordered it in for a St Andrew's Day Scottish cheese feature. In retail we are sometimes guilty of playing to the public holidays from around the world to give variety to our displays and to give focus. I had never tried Anster, but it was one of a handful of Scottish cheeses available for me to purchase, so that is how our relationship began.

It is a cheese made by Jane Stewart in Fife, where Jane's husband and his family have been farming since the 1930s. In 2008 they started their journey into cheesemaking. Jane had the opportunity to learn how to make cheese with a maker in Wales who was just about to go into retirement. His crumbly cheese became the inspiration for Anster, as this was the first style that she was shown how to make in a real dairy environment.

Anster is a firm, crumbly cheese using techniques from the north of England. It is aged between two to four months, as certain cheeses need a little longer to mature to the profile the makers desire, and they use four different starter cultures. Anster has a beautiful, delicate milky flavour and crumble, and refined yogurt acidity.

Semi-Hard

If you like Anster, you'll also like Wensleydale.

FLAVOUR
BUTTER

Butter on its own is one of my favourite food groups. I adore slathering butter on toast. In a restaurant the butter in the dish on the table is enough for one mouthful, so I usually end up asking to buy several more.

Buttery flavours in cheeses are very pleasing and generally appear in milder cheeses or as one isolated flavour profile among many in more complex cheeses. My favourite iteration of butter is in Lancashire cheese, and most specifically in Kirkham's Lancashire cheese. I'm certain that Lancashire's father is butter as it is that integral to its genes. This cheese has what the maker's family call a 'buttery crumble', with a delicious mouthful of butter and yogurt in each bite.

I enjoy a particular butter flavour in cheeses such as Asiago (page 114) and Havarti (page 115). These are cheeses that, when young, have simple, cultured-butter and yogurt notes. Their chubby, springy textures add to this overall experience because their fatty pastes coat the mouth and when you bite them, you can leave teeth marks, like in a firm pat of butter.

There is an organic compound called diacetyl, which produces a buttery aroma and flavour, and it comes out frequently in fermented foods, as it is naturally produced by lactic acid bacteria. Diacetyl is responsible for some of the buttery flavours found in cheeses. Diacetyl gets a bad press for being 'bad for you', however, this is when it is inhaled (in vaping, for instance) but not when it is ingested.

Semi-Hard

ORIGIN: Somerset, England

FLAVOUR NOTES: Butter, vegetal, earthy

PAIRS WELL WITH: A Pinot Blanc like Elk Cove Vineyards
Willamette Valley Estate, or a mild ale

Ogleshield

(Unpasteurised, Cows' Milk, Traditional Rennet)

Every other year at the Slow Food Cheese Festival in Bra, Italy, a cheese maturer hosts an evening soirée of sorts for his customers and like-minded folks. I was honoured to have been invited to this on my first year at Bra, which also happened to be the time when Ogleshield was served to everyone for dinner as a Raclette alternative. Brilliant.

It is a washed-rind cheese made in North Cadbury by Jamie Montgomery. Unlike the Montgomery's Cheddar, Ogleshield is made exclusively using Jersey milk from their Jersey cattle herd. This wasn't always a washed-rind cheese – it was the idea of Bill Oglethorpe, a cheesemaker in London who was, at the time, the head maturer at Neal's Yard Dairy. He suggested, based on his cheesemaking training in the Alps, that washing the rind of the cheese would allow for it to store and mature differently. Thanks to him, this cheese recipe was born and, to nod to this contribution, the name of the cheese, which was then Jersey Shield, was changed to Ogleshield, named by the Neal's Yard Dairy wholesale team.

Ogleshield is a similar style to Raclette and other alpine melting cheeses. It is buttery, savoury and pliable in texture. A fabulous melter, this is best enjoyed in a toastie or slathered all over waxy potatoes.

Semi-Hard

If you like Ogleshield, you'll also like Raclette.

ORIGIN: Lancashire, England

FLAVOUR NOTES: Butter, lemony, acid

PAIRS WELL WITH: A Sauvignon Blanc, Daiginjo saké, or a Strawberry Margarita

Lancashire

(Unpasteurised, Cows' Milk, Traditional Rennet)

There is a raw-milk, farmhouse Lancashire cheese made by Graham Kirkham that I love so much that my colleague and I once decided to purchase 13 wheels of it to sell over a weekend at Whole Foods Market, just for fun. I will never, ever get bored of this cheese.

Lancashire cheese is now made in both factory and farmhouse guises, whereas in the past it would have been solely farmhouse in the nineteenth and twentieth centuries. This would have been a very slow make and the result of the mixing of several days' worth of curd, as many small farms wouldn't have had enough milk from their small number of animals to make an entire cheese from one day's yield.

There are two main types of Lancashire – creamy and tasty – and most recently added, in the mid-twentieth century, is crumbly, to account for the faster, industrial make that is most widespread nowadays and whose speed results in a more dramatic crumble. There is just one maker of raw-milk Lancashire cheese now, Kirkham's Lancashire, and it is an outstanding cheese, which I urge you to seek out. Kirkham's Lancashire is buttery, creamy, warming and delicious as is, but is also the best for cheese on toast and super tasty alongside apple pie. The crumbly Lancashire is like the other industrially made British crumblies, with a high acidity, lemon note and crumble.

Semi-Hard

If you like Kirkham's Lancashire, you like excellent cheese!

ORIGIN: Veneto and Trento, Italy

FLAVOUR NOTES: Yogurt, butter, fruity

PAIRS WELL WITH: A light and fruity red wine like Schiava,
a lager like Pilsner Urquell, or lemonade

Asiago DOP

(Unpasteurised, Cows' Milk, Traditional Rennet or Vegetarian Coagulant)

Asiago is my ideal hangover cheese. I used to love eating this if I had a
big night the night before. There is something very comforting about a
wedge of young Asiago to get me back on my feet again.

Asiago is one of the oldest Italian cheeses, with Greek and Latin
texts mentioning dairy production in the area of Veneto; around the year
1000 CE, there was documentation of a cheese from the Asiago plateau.

Asiago is a large ivory wheel weighing in at around 10 to 15kg.
There are two main distinctions of Asiago under the DOP – Asiago
Fresco (young/fresh) and Asiago Stagionato (aged). Asiago can be made
with either traditional rennet from an animal, or a thistle coagulant. The
younger cheeses have a beautiful yogurt flavour as well as flavours of
buttered, freshly baked bread. The cheese has characteristic 'eyes',
which are small, irregular holes throughout the paste, and its aroma is of
fresh milk, lemon and cream. The Stagionato cheese is categorised
according to increments of ageing. These aged cheeses have a lot more
bite and tang, with fruity and peppery flavours lacing them.

Semi-Hard

If you like Asiago DOP, you'll also like Havarti.

ORIGIN: Nationwide, Denmark

FLAVOUR NOTES: Yogurt, butter, tangy

PAIRS WELL WITH: A Provence rosé like Mirabeau Classic
Provence Rosé, or a Junmai Ginjo saké

Havarti

(Pasteurised, Cows' Milk, Traditional Rennet)

Havarti is another of my favourite hangover cheeses. Its simplicity and yogurt sour are very comforting to me when feeling a little peaky. This cheese is named after the farm in Denmark where the cheese was created by cheesemaker Hanne Nielsen. Hanne travelled around Europe learning cheesemaking skills and when she decided upon making this cheese, she named it after her farm in Havarthigaard, north of Copenhagen.

Although there are versions made in the USA and Canada, the original comes from Denmark, so look for this when you are purchasing, as the styles will differ. Danish Havarti comes in a block format, like a long loaf of bread. The cheese has an elastic paste and lots of holes lacing it throughout. The flavour is very comforting. It has a light, milky aroma and a simple flavour range on the palate. It is yogurty, buttery and makes for a very good transitional cheese for those looking to come out of their Cheddar comfort zone. It is a good melter, and I adore it in a toastie or a simple sandwich.

Semi-Hard

If you like Havarti, you'll also like Asiago DOP.

FLAVOUR
SMOKED

Smoked cheeses now predominantly undertake this process for flavour. But smoking traditionally has further purpose – it is a method of preservation seen in many types of food for two main reasons. Firstly, smoking dehydrates food, be it fish, meat or cheese. By removing moisture, it allows a product to last longer – moisture is the key factor for food perishing. Secondly, smoking covers a cheese in acidic compounds that create a hostile environment against the growth of bacteria or fungi.

Smoking adds flavour to cheeses, and this has now become a desired enhancement. The popularity of smoked cheeses is so apparent that some cheeses are now enhanced with liquid smoke to cheat the process. This is an artificial way of smoking, and its flavour can taste artificial too, so look out for this in the ingredients when you are buying a cheese, and try to opt for cheeses that have been prepared with real smoke instead. Sometimes smoking is said to be a 'cover-up', used to fix batches of cheese which are subpar, but it can, when done properly, achieve a very desirable flavour profile.

Cheeses are generally cold-smoked so as not to create a molten, gooey, smoky mess. One cheesemaker in the UK has even transformed an old phone box into a smoking chamber! The cheeses in this section are recipes from around the world, and you will see that you can smoke any style of cheese. Smoked Cheddar and other hard cheeses are the most popular in style. I have really enjoyed a smoked blue before, but my absolute favourite was a fresh ewes'-milk cheese, like a goats'-milk Crottin de Chavignol in style, which I tasted on a farm in Normandy. I have never, and will never, forget that cheese.

Semi-Hard

ORIGIN: Podhale, Poland

FLAVOUR NOTES: Smoky, animal, salty

PAIRS WELL WITH: A Baltic porter, a Lingonberry mocktail or simply a shot of good quality vodka

Oscypek

(Unpasteurised, Ewes' Milk, Traditional Rennet)

Oscypek is one of the most beautiful cheeses I have ever come across. It is shaped like a spindle, with an intricate design on its surface, brought out even further by the gentle orange and brown hues from the smoking process.

Everything about the production of this cheese is gorgeous, including the location. It is a ewes'-milk cheese made in the Tatra mountains, which border Slovakia. The cheese is made seasonally, and, during this time, the ewes are brought up to higher pastures, between 80 and 1,500m above sea level. The cheese is made in wooden huts called *bacówka*, where a group of cheesemakers work together making the cheese, forming and smoking it. The raw milk from the morning is added into the milk from the previous evening. This is then heated in a copper cauldron over an open wood fire and once the curds have formed, they are transferred into a wooden barrel filled with hot water. The cheeses are placed here to make the paste malleable in order to form into its unique spindle shape. To finish, they have their intricate patterns pressed around using a wooden stamp clamp.

The flavours in Oscypek are smoky, animal and salty. It is typically eaten grilled or in thin slices alongside a lingonberry preserve.

Semi-Hard

If you like Oscypek, you'll also like Scamorza.

Chechil

(Pasteurised, Cows', Ewes' or Goats' Milk,
Acid Coagulation [Vegetarian])

Chechil is a string cheese made using the same method of the stretched-curd (pasta-filata) cheeses we saw earlier in the book, like Quesillo (page 21). Unlike Quesillo, which has long, thick ropey strands, Chechil is formed into very thin strands worked together to make a plait. It is made in Armenia, and also in neighbouring Georgia. It is known under several names, including 'husats' and 'tel', and can sometimes be enhanced with nigella seeds or marjoram.

The milk is pre-ripened for approximately three hours before it is transformed into cheese. The whey is not drained off, and the curd is gathered and formed into a mass while still in its whey; here, it is stretched into strands and formed into a plait.

There is a blue version of Chechil, which is the strangest cheese I have ever encountered. It looks like torn chicken breast (not formed into a plait) and blue moulds are encouraged to grow in abundance. The cheese looks like a creation you would like to keep as far away from your mouth as possible, but it tastes surprisingly smooth. If you ever stumble across it, I'd recommend giving it a go. If you are feeling brave, Chechil in all its variations is a little chewy, salty and gently smoked, making a great snack, especially with an alcoholic drink.

Semi-Hard

If you like Chechil, you'll also like Scamorza.

ORIGIN: Puglia and Calabria, Italy

FLAVOUR NOTES: Smoky, salty, milky

PAIRS WELL WITH: A red wine such as Syrah/Shiraz, Dunkel beer, or a Negroni

Scamorza Affumicata

(Pasteurised, Cows' Milk, Traditional Rennet)

Scamorza is a Southern Italian cheese. The smoked version of this cheese is the Scamorza Affumicata (smoked). It is shaped like a pear, similarly to Provolone. It has a tight, smooth paste and a golden hue to its exterior for the more commercially produced and a coating resembling dark ash wood for the more traditional. Scamorza is said to have its origins in Puglia and Calabria, but now you can see it made in a wider area across Southern Italy.

I adore Scamorza Affumicata. I am not a huge fan of overly smoked flavours in cheeses, as many can taste quite acidic and like you are eating an ash tray. Scamorza Affumicata is relatively gently smoked. It is a pasta filata style of cheese like the Oscypek (page 117) and others like Quesillo (page 21). Scamorza looks like a bouncy ball of Mozzarella, and this is the only smoked cheese where I prefer the smoked version to its original.

It's a fabulous melting cheese, frequently baked in a cast-iron or other ovenproof dish and eaten as a molten dip with bruschetta and salad. It is also great in a risotto, grilled with lemon leaves.

Semi-Hard

If you like Scamorza, why not try Oscypek?

ORIGIN: Bavaria, Germany

FLAVOUR NOTES: Smoky, milky, buttery

PAIRS WELL WITH: Red wines like Blaufränkisch,
a stout like the Wild Beer Co. Millionaire Milk Stout,
or a Bourbon

Rauchkäse

(Pasteurised, Cows' Milk, Traditional Rennet)

Rauchkäse simply translates as 'smoked cheese', and there are a wealth of these cheeses hailing from Bavaria in Germany. This is a processed cheese, so it is not 100 per cent cheese (it is cheese plus extra ingredients – cheese diluted, if you will). The extra ingredients generally consist of emulsifiers, butter or other dairy products and preservatives, with the common ground of making a product that could resist a nuclear bomb, like a cheesy cockroach. The creation of processed cheeses is a technology that began in Switzerland in the early twentieth century. They are made by melting down a base cheese – in this case, a Bavarian Emmental-style cheese – and blending it with further ingredients before re-forming it into a solid mass. Although this is not what I would call 'real cheese', it is a process which uses modern technology to extend the life of a product for preservation, in a very cheap way.

There is a Rauchkäse made by a company called Bergader, which started its journey in 1902. It is cold-smoked over Bavarian beech and spruce woodchips to give its distinct, gentle smoked flavour.

These cheeses are useful for melting and make cheap alternatives that will sit in your fridge forever, to appear when you most need them (at 3am after a night out or when your other cheese is all gone).

Semi-Hard

If you like Rauchkäse, you'll also like Scamorza.

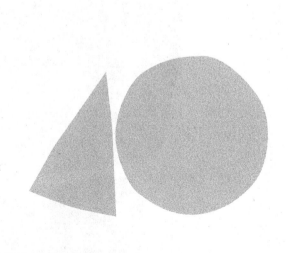

Hard

Five

What do we mean by a 'hard cheese'? Semantically, this can mean many things. A goats' cheese such as Crottin de Chavignol can be aged and dried, making its texture tricky to cut with a knife, so it is a hard version of a soft recipe! A cheese left unwrapped and drying out in the elements will also lose fats and oils, becoming hard. In this chapter, we are looking at cheeses that have undergone specific processes in the way they are made, to become intentionally 'hard' cheeses.

Let's think about texture. Parmigiano Reggiano (page 142), Cheddar (page 144), Gouda (page 149) and Gruyère (page 145) are all firm cheeses with a very low moisture content. However, they all begin with milk, which is wet with all the moisture content. So, in the process of making hard cheeses, we want to separate the milk into curds and whey, as with all makes, but this time we want to remove more moisture from the curd than we would with a soft cheese. Methods to do this include cutting the curd size into very small pieces, heating these pieces of curd and pressing the cheese, all methods for a drier, firmer finished product.

These techniques allow the cheeses to last longer and to be aged longer. Comté, for instance, is made at a high altitude in the summer, with limited access for travel, so the milk is used to make a cheese that can be stored, unlike a young cheese, which needs to be sold quickly. Because of this longer storage, prices are generally higher. The cheese needs a place to live, and people to care for it. Cheese cannot simply be left and aged – it needs controlled conditions and people who know how to do this. It needs both a cheese mortgage and staff added to its cost. Some cheeses have specialist maturers, also known as affineurs, who specialise in the controlled care and development of a cheese from as early in the process as the cheese being removed from its mould.

Not all cheeses age well and not all cheeses which age well, age well. Confusing, right? Not all Comté cheeses are destined to be long aged, for example, as they need to be regularly tested and graded to make sure they have the right flavour profile, texture and acidity. If they do not have these prerequisites for longer ageing, they are eaten at a younger age.

Hard cheeses are texturally ideal for grating. For example, outside of its native Italy, Parmigiano Reggiano is rarely seen on a cheeseboard. It's viewed as more of a commodity, which is a travesty! Parmigiano Reggiano absolutely deserves to be on a cheeseboard and really should be. Its grating and flavour-enhancing properties are a bonus. It is filled with flavours of umami which we know and love in many other hard cheeses and it pairs perfectly with a range of drinks and accompaniments. Flavour complexity develops with age, and you find flavours which do not exist in younger cheeses, owing to the breakdown of proteins. This breakdown can also form the crystals we enjoy crunching in long-aged cheese.

The four flavours in this chapter are not a finite list – they are four common flavours which, for me, stand out the most in hard cheeses. If you were to look at a Comté tasting wheel, you would see hundreds of descriptors for just this one cheese, so, once again, use these as a starting point to guide you into finding your own flavours!

FLAVOUR
ANIMAL

Here we are looking at truly wild flavours seen in cheeses that are traditional in both their production method and their flavours. In this section we look at Salers, a cheese whose production methods would give any Environmental Health Officer in the UK a myocardial infarction: microbial information translating into flavour from calves' saliva on the teats, milk interacting with the wooden barrel in which it is made, and all the delicious bacteria. Some of these cheeses are wild, funky and very hard to pinpoint in their exact flavour profiles, as they change so frequently. These cheeses have strong animal, meaty, farmy, herbaceous and vegetal flavours. If you find these cheeses, give them a try. They are not the most widely distributed, so you may not locate these as easily as others listed in the book. They are most certainly not for everyone, but I urge you to try them and appreciate their place in the broadest context of cheese.

In this 'animal' section, at one end of the spectrum you have Salers (page 128) and at the other you have Manchego (page 132). Manchego's flavours are a little more straight-laced and accessible, and with cooked meat flavours like lamb chops. Pecorino Sardo has a strong connection with the animal flavours of the ewes' milk they are made from, but with a more gentle, cooked meat approach. Salers is a wild rock star. Its flavours are raw, primal and animalistic. See overleaf for more.

Hard

Salers AOP

(Unpasteurised, Cows' Milk, Traditional Rennet)

Where do I begin with this cheese? It is an Environmental Health Officer's worst nightmare and a microbiologist's dream. It is made using wooden equipment that is not cleaned at all with conventional chemicals during the season in which it is made. Salers is a very old, traditional recipe, an incredibly wild-tasting cheese which does not allow you to forget where it comes from: cows.

The milk used to make this cheese comes from cows of the same name – the Salers breed. The cows are out on pasture for the entire season, and this must happen for the cheese to adhere to the AOP regulations. Unfortunately, in 2022, with the extreme droughts in France, Salers production had to be ceased early in the season as there was simply not enough pasture for the cows to graze on. Salers animal husbandry is the epitome of ethical dairy. The cows must have their calves with them when they give their milk – and this does not happen in a milking parlour. There are mobile milking stations which come out to the cows in the field. The calves must start to suckle before the mother releases milk, and once the calf has had its share, the farmers are able to switch in and collect the milk. These cows can be cheeky, though! When I was visiting a Salers herd in the Auvergne, I witnessed a mother who had kept back some milk for her calf. She 'switched off' her milk supply for the farmer and when her calf went back to suckling, it was covered in a milky bath.

Salers is a wonderfully expressive cheese. Although texturally comparable to a British cheese, its flavours speak a different language.

Salers starts off in familiar territory, with some grassy and spicy flavours reminiscent of a mature British farmhouse cheese before heading into barny, animal, earthy and acidic.

Hard

If you like Salers AOP, you may also like Farmhouse Cheddar.

ORIGIN: Auvergne, France

FLAVOUR NOTES: Animal, brothy, farmy

PAIRS WELL WITH: A Chardonnay like Côtes d'Auvergne Blanc,
a golden ale, or a dry perry

Cantal AOP

(Unpasteurised, Cows' Milk, Traditional Rennet)

Did Cantal come before Cheddar or did Cheddar come before Cantal? There are several theories, and they all need more than this page allows, but it is a curious thing that these cheeses both follow very similar make processes despite being so far away from each other.

Cantal is a large-format drum sitting at around the 40kg mark. It has a natural rind which is a grey/brown colour. Cantal is pressed twice: once to break up the curd again, and then it is salted before being pressed a second time. These stages are important for the cheeses' flavour and texture characteristics.

There are three types of Cantal sold, differentiated by age.

1. Cantal Jeune (the youngest age profile of the cheese) is aged between 30 to 60 days and it is fresh, milky and fruity.
2. Cantal Entre Deux is aged between three to six months. Here, you will find notes of butter, cream, dairy and hay.
3. Cantal Vieux is the name for the age profile thereafter. Here, you will find wild, salty and gamey deliciousness. I have on many occasions tasted banana and tropical fruits in younger cheeses and more animal, vegetal and ramen-soup flavours in these older cheeses. This type is my favourite as no two pieces seem to taste the same.

There is a dish from this region called aligot, which is one of my desert island dishes. It is essentially mashed potatoes with young Cantal mixed in, and is typically served with charcuterie.

Hard

If you like Cantal AOP, you'll also like Cheddar.

ORIGIN: Sardinia, Italy

FLAVOUR NOTES: Animal, grassy, spicy

PAIRS WELL WITH: A white wine such as Vernaccia di Oristano,
a Mezcal Margarita, or oolong tea

Pecorino Sardo DOP

(Unpasteurised or Thermised, Ewes' Milk, Traditional Rennet)

'Pecorino' is a term used for many different types of ewes'-milk cheeses from Italy. *'Pecora'* means sheep in Italian and so the word is derived from this. Pecorino as a term on its own is not protected and can refer to many varieties of ewes' milk cheese. The most common is Pecorino Romano, which is used world over and is integral to the dish cacio e pepe, a simple yet delicious pasta dish, literally translating as 'cheese' and 'pepper'.

Pecorino Sardo comes from Sardinia, which has very specific climatic conditions as an island, all of which contribute to the flavour profile of Pecorino Sardo. There are two types of Pecorino Sardo: Dolce (sweet) or Maturo (mature). Where many cheeses of differing ages are just separated by the number of months they are matured, Pecorino Sardo has a distinction in the process itself. The curd size is cut differently, the mature cheese having its curd pieces cut to a smaller size to allow for more whey expulsion and to mature for longer without the moisture there as a factor for it perishing. They are also made in slightly different sizes and moulds to differentiate them. In the Dolce, the flavours are sweet, mild and grassy, where in the Maturo they are more animal, fruity and spicy.

Hard

If you like Pecorino Sardo DOP, you'll also like
Yorkshire Pecorino Fiore.

ORIGIN: Nationwide, Croatia

FLAVOUR NOTES: Animal, tangy, salty

PAIRS WELL WITH: An orange wine, a cider,
or white vermouth on the rocks

Sir iz mišine

(Unpasteurised, Ewes' Milk, Traditional Rennet)

Sir iz mišine is a cheese which is matured and presented in a sheep skin. It is quite something to look at. This is a cheese traditionally made in Croatia, but there are many different types of cheeses matured in skins/sacks around the Balkans. The sack is a complete sheep skin coming from a one- to two-year-old sheep. The skins are prepared, hung and dried in the early months of the year, and later on, when the milk is plentiful, cheese is made and put into the sacks. The best versions of the cheese is when there is enough salted curd in one sitting to fill an entire sack. When the farms have less milk and make less cheese, they need to use multiple makes over several days to fill an entire sack. This means that the ageing process is disrupted and the ages of the different batches of curd will be slightly different.

The cheese looks like a dry, crumbly Feta style. It is a little salty, slightly animal but with a delicious tang.

Hard

If you like Sir iz mišine, you'll also like an aged Feta.

ORIGIN: La Mancha, Spain

FLAVOUR NOTES: Animal, briny, nutty

PAIRS WELL WITH: A Tempranillo-based wine like Condado
de Haza Ribera Del Duero, Amontillado sherry,
or a Lambic beer

Manchego DOP

(Unpasteurised and Pasteurised, Ewes' Milk,
Traditional and Vegetarian Rennet)

If you ask someone to name a Spanish cheese, the chances are they will say Manchego. It is an incredibly popular cheese for many reasons. Manchego is always made using ewes' milk from the Manchega breed of sheep. The DOP is split into two types: Manchego and Manchego Artisano, which are very different beasts. Manchego Artisano can only be made using raw milk and, although it isn't enforced, many of these producers are of a smaller scale. Traditional rennet is used for this recipe as it is said to give a fuller, richer flavour. Manchego without 'Artisano' after its name is made with pasteurised milk and vegetarian rennet. Pre-DOP, there would have been many more variations of this cheese in areas outside of La Mancha.

A good-quality Manchego will give aromas of dry pasture, and flavours can show green olive, pineapple, untoasted almonds and hazelnuts, rounded off with a sheepy, animal finish. I love to eat it as is, with a little olive oil and bread, and it works very well with the simple pan con tomate (tomato bread) or on a cheese plate with raisins, dried nuts and fruits, or pickled figs.

Hard

If you like Manchego DOP, you'll also like Zamorano DOP.

ORIGIN: Wisconsin, USA

FLAVOUR NOTES: Animal, earthy, nutty

PAIRS WELL WITH: Bourbon, a brown ale such as Newcastle, or an Oloroso sherry

Dunbarton Blue

(Pasteurised, Cows' Milk, Traditional Rennet)

No, I haven't lost my mind and put this is the wrong section; this is one of the cheeses I mentioned in my introduction that can sit in multiple categories. This is a hybrid cheese made by Roelli Cheese Haus in Wisconsin. Cheesemaker Chris Roelli's two favourite cheese styles are Cheddar and Blue, so, as you do, he decided to put them together!

You will see natural but unintentional blue veins appearing in clothbound Cheddars; however, in Dunbarton Blue this is fully intentional. Chris makes his Cheddar-style cheeses, presses them and then pierces them. This creates slim channels for the blue moulds to navigate, so it is clear where the needles have pierced the cheese, as the lines of blue are so uniform.

Dunbarton Blue is a savoury, nutty and earthy hard cheese, with the blue moulds complementing this and not overpowering. The blueing is present but subtle. Its natural rind is distinctly reminiscent of a British clothbound Cheddar and its cave-ageing most certainly plays a part in this role of flavour development.

Hard

If you like Dunbarton Blue, you'll also like traditional clothbound Cheddar.

FLAVOUR
SPICY

'Spicy' is a term we use for cheeses which are deemed 'strong'. 'Peppery' and 'piquant' are also terms you will hear time and time again referring to certain hard cheeses and many blue cheeses. So, what do they have in common?

These are all long-aged cheeses which have been subjected to a lot of breakdown. No, they do not need to see a counsellor, they are fine in that respect, but because of their age, they have seen a lot of action from their degradation pathways. There are three degradation pathways that you see in cheese. These are lipolysis (breakdown of fat), glycolysis (breakdown of sugar) and proteolysis (breakdown of protein). These all play their parts in the maturing and affinage of cheese and they can be both incredibly positive texturally and in flavour – but if they go too far, they will start to tip over the edge into the unmanageable in texture and undesirable in flavour.

Lipolysis leads to the creation of small, short-chain fatty acids called butyric acid. This is responsible for a lot of the characteristics we find in these spicy cheeses. There is a highly appealing term that we use as cheesemongers called 'baby vomit', which gives that typical piquant, spicy flavour. In moderation and at the right stage, this is a desirable flavour, but in excess, not so great. This free fatty acid is not the only factor responsible for the spice in these cheeses, but it comes up frequently as a common denominator.

ORIGIN: Serra da Canastra, Minas Gerais, Brazil

FLAVOUR NOTES: Spicy, animal, savoury

PAIRS WELL WITH: Prosecco, a German Helles beer, or cachaça

Canastra

(Unpasteurised, Cows' Milk, Traditional Rennet)

Canastra is a traditional raw-milk cheese made in several provinces of Brazil, including Bambui, Delfinópolis and Medeiros. This artisanal cheese has been made since the Portuguese colonial settlers came to the land in the beginning of the eighteenth century. It is a very 'local' cheese, with all parts of its production taking place in the area. The milk comes from nearby livestock, and they are predominantly raised on pasture. For the most traditional producers, the native grass species are integral to producing a high-quality cheese.

The cheese, although pressed and hard, is eaten very young, at a minimum of 21 days. Longer ageing is more popular these days. In 2008, The National Historic and Artistic Heritage Institute (IPHAN) recognised Canastra as a historical, cultural heritage of Brazil. To this end, the government financed the construction of collective ageing rooms for the producers to long age their cheeses. Typically, they are matured in cheese rooms attached to the producers' homes.

Canastra undergoes very natural production methods with low intervention. The raw milk uses starter cultures called 'pingo', which are whey starters taken from the previous day's make. It's predominantly female-led in its production. Flavours are full and rich, cooked and warming, with similarities to those such as Grana Padano (page 143).

Hard

If you like Canastra, you'll also like Grana Padano DOP.

ORIGIN: Västerbotten, Sweden

FLAVOUR NOTES: Spicy, fruity, salty

PAIRS WELL WITH: A mature Chianti, red ale, or aquavit

Västerbottensost

(Pasteurised, Cows' Milk, Traditional Rennet)

Västerbottensost is a hard cheese from Sweden. Like Parmigiano Reggiano (page 142) and Grana Padano (page 143), its texture is granular, and it has a firmness, small holes, and crystals throughout. It is a cheese which has been made since the late 1800s. I was lucky enough to try this a few years back when a Swedish colleague brought some back from his trip home. It is not just sold in Sweden – you can find it across the globe.

It is aged for at least 14 months (five months longer than the minimum age for a Grana Padano, for reference) and its character develops considerably in this time frame. There is a Gouda-esque sweetness and bite to the cheese as well as a slight vegetal bitterness and a warm, heated-up-milk flavour within.

There is an excellent tradition in Sweden of crayfish parties in August. I am all for any culture that has shellfish parties. One of the dishes eaten is Västerbottensostpaj, a flan of sorts using this tasty cheese.

Hard

136

**If you like Västerbottensost, you'll also like
Parmigiano Reggiano DOP.**

ORIGIN: Northern Italy

FLAVOUR NOTES: Umami, spicy, fruity

PAIRS WELL WITH: A Pinot Grigio, a Dunkel beer like
Erdinger Dunkel, or a Virgin Berry Blast

Provolone Valpadana DOP

(Unpasteurised, Cows' Milk, Traditional Rennet)

The name 'Provolone' is unprotected, so, in theory, can be made anywhere. Here, we are looking at Provolone Valpadana DOP, of which there are two varieties – Dolce and Piccante. This cheese has its protected designation of origin (DOP), meaning that all the stages of production and ageing must be undertaken in the stipulated area. Starter cultures, like in other Italian cheeses such as Parmigiano Reggiano (page 142), must come from the previous day's whey. The two varieties have different sensory properties and differences in their make. The mild version (Dolce) is made using calf rennet, with a percentage of kid or lamb rennet permitted. For the strong version (Piccante), the rennet must come from a kid or a lamb.

The Dolce has an elastic paste and aromas of milk and butter. On the palate it is salty, fruity, lactic, vegetal and umami, many of the flavours you find in cooked foods. In contrast, the Piccante has much more complexity on the nose, where it is more animal and fruitier. On the palate you can find cooked dairy, umami and a lot of spice at the finish.

Hard

**If you like Provolone Valpadana DOP, you'll also
like Pecorino Sardo.**

ORIGIN: Lincolnshire, England

FLAVOUR NOTES: Spicy, tropical, sweet

PAIRS WELL WITH: A Cabernet Sauvignon or
Bordeaux blend red wines, an ale, or a cider

Lincolnshire Poacher

(Unpasteurised, Cows' Milk, Traditional Rennet)

Lincolnshire Poacher was one of my first favourite cheeses for years when I started out as a cheesemonger.

Lincolnshire Poacher is a British cheese that could be mistaken for a Cheddar on appearance alone. It is a large truckle, like a Cheddar, and on visually inspecting its rind and paste, it could still be. However, its texture is different because of the method of making the cheese. Where a Cheddar is 'Cheddared' and the blocks of curd are stacked on top of each other to expel moisture, this does not happen in Lincolnshire Poacher, where the curd blocks are merely rested upon one another. There are various other differences in the make which give it a more waxy, firmer texture, skewing towards an Alpine in style. The minimum ageing is 15 months in order for this flavour and texture to develop fully.

Its nose is fruity, tropical and a bit earthy on the rind. On the palate, it frequently has an undeniable flavour of pineapple throughout, as well as warm, cooked notes, dairy, grass and hay. This is a beautiful cheese that I would highly recommend if you're a Cheddar fan looking for something similar, or a hard-cheese fan looking for something with a great fruity profile and a bit of a bite.

Hard

**If you like Lincolnshire Poacher, you'll also like
Isle of Mull Cheddar.**

ORIGIN: São Jorge, Portugal

FLAVOUR NOTES: Animal, spicy, nutty

PAIRS WELL WITH: A Palo Cortado sherry, a dark ale like
Adnams Broadside, or a mocktail like Apple Highball from Seedlip

São Jorge DOP

(Unpasteurised, Cows' Milk, Traditional Rennet)

São Jorge DOP is a Portuguese cheese which must be made exclusively on the stunning island of São Jorge in the Azores, a good 900 miles from the west coast of mainland Portugal. It is a hard cheese made exclusively using raw milk and fermented using whey starters. It is said to have originated from a Flemish settler who brought Dutch cheesemaking knowledge to the island. The climate here creates a highly fertile soil, which grows pasture that is perfect for cattle to graze upon. The island is very humid and the soil is volcanic, elements which create this fecundity.

On the nose São Jorge is animal, wild, herby and peppery. On the palate it is similar, with an acidity and sourness that develops with its ageing. Locally, it is eaten as a dessert with banana or jam as an accompaniment, which sounds a little off-piste, but salt/savoury and sweet always work well together. I find this cheese very powerful, animal and with a big acidic bite. It isn't the first cheese that springs to my mind when thinking of dessert cheeses, but this is the joy of regional cuisine!

Hard

**If you like São Jorge DOP, you'll also like
Parmigiano Reggiano DOP.**

ORIGIN: Deichkäse, Germany

FLAVOUR NOTES: Spicy, nutty, fruity

PAIRS WELL WITH: A dark rum such as
Dos Maderas 5+5 PX, or a wheat beer

Deichkäse

(Unpasteurised, Cows' Milk, Traditional Rennet)

'Deichkäse' translates from German to 'dyke/dam cheese', as the dairy that makes it is near to the dikes in the Frisia region along the North Sea. Since 2022 the farm has started creating its own renewable energy from both solar panels and biogas, allowing them to fuel their farm as well as over 2,000 further households.

The cheeses, made by two brothers under the diary name Backensholzer Hof, are produced on their own farm, which has, since 1991, been certified by Bioland, the largest organic food association in Germany. Their mother's motto 'the cheesemaking begins in the field' encapsulates their ethos: that a great cheese needs a solid foundation of healthy animals, good feed and good milk in order to taste great.

Deichkäse comes in various age profiles, from four months up to 18+ months. As the cheese ages, it develops a spicy, animal character concentrated in flavour. You can eat it in small pieces and still receive a taste explosion in every bite. The cheese at this age also lends itself well to being used in cooking, as it becomes an aged umami bomb.

Hard

If you like Deichkäse, you'll also like São Jorge DOP.

FLAVOUR
UMAMI

Fermented products have a high concentration of umami in their flavour spectrum. We are looking at hard cheeses in this section, cheeses which have undergone a long maturation and have a low moisture content. When cheese matures, milk proteins break down into free amino acids and the longer a cheese matures, the more this happens. Proteins do not have flavour, but when broken down into amino acids, the flavour party begins. The amino acid responsible for umami flavour is glutamate, which you find frequently in hard, long-aged cheeses and blues.

This is why you see umami appear in many hard cheeses, such as Parmigiano Reggiano (page 142) and Cheddar, as well as blues like Roquefort (page 160). These cheeses have all undergone long maturation, and therefore, the complexity of these cheeses is much broader than in softer, younger and non-aged cheeses.

This complexity and umami 'deliciousness' is the reason why we use these cheeses atop dishes and why only a little bit is needed to give a huge impact (although it is much more fun to use lots of cheese). Umami is an addictive flavour which taps into our primal brain. As with bitter tastes being indicative of poisonous foods, umami is a flavour we crave because it is an indicator that there is protein in the foods that we are eating.

Hard

ORIGIN: Emilia Romagna, Italy

FLAVOUR NOTES: Umami, nutty, fruity

PAIRS WELL WITH: Red wines like an Amarone della Valpolicella Classico, an imperial stout, or a whisky matured in old sherry barrels like Auchentoshan Three Wood

Parmigiano Reggiano DOP

(Unpasteurised, Cows' Milk, Traditional Rennet)

Parmigiano Reggiano is a cheese known throughout the world. There are imitations of this cheese, but the true cheese holds a DOP, and it is made and matured in Emilia-Romagna. For those of you who haven't seen a whole wheel before, it is a gigantic 40kg drum which has a smaller diameter and taller height than the similarly enormous Beaufort. Its authenticity is indicated by a number of markings on the rind.

Its origins lie in the Middle Ages, and we can thank the Benedictine and Cistercian monks for its creation. They sought to make a cheese that would last. Using milk from the cows on the farms they owned, along with techniques using salt from the Salsomaggiore mines, they developed the beginnings of the recipe we know and love today.

Parmigiano Reggiano is underutilised outside of Italy. We employ it for cooking – in recipes and as a seasoning – for which its use is well deserved. I am a firm believer that you should use the best ingredients to make the best meals. We must remember, however, that Parmigiano Reggiano is not just a condiment but also a wonderful, long-aged cheesy masterpiece which deserves to sit on a cheeseboard.

It is umami in the medium of cheese, with tropical fruit, salt, and a crystalline texture.

Hard

If you like Parmigiano Reggiano DOP, why not try Grana Padano DOP?

FLAVOUR NOTES: Savoury, grassy, sweet

PAIRS WELL WITH: Red wines like Brunello di Montalcino,
a pale ale, or an Aperol Spritz

Grana Padano DOP

(Unpasteurised, Cows' Milk, Traditional Rennet)

As with so many old traditional recipes, our trusty friends the monks are responsible for the development of this recipe. Grana Padano has a very similar form to other Grana-style cheeses in that it is enormous, very hard and long-aged, and it has a thick, yellow rind created from the brining process.

Its texture is granular, which is where the name Grana (grain) comes into play. When the cheese is made, the curds are cut to a very small size, which allows for the removal of moisture, necessary for long-ageing cheeses, especially those of this size. Grana Padano weight boundaries are quite extreme, with a minimum of 24kg and with some cheeses weighing up to 40kg.

Its flavour is complex, as the cheese is aged for a minimum of nine months. The grainy texture shatters when cut, but it still holds enough moisture to allow a giving, and not a dry, mouthfeel. The rind is fully natural and edible. You can grate it down and use it as you would a grated cheese or you can use it in cooking as a cheesy stock cube. I recently saw a chef creating the most beautiful-looking Grana-rind 'chicharron' (typically fried pork belly or rinds), so there is a lot of room for being creative. Flavours are fruity, milky and sweet.

Hard

**If you like Grana Padano DOP,
you will like Parmigiano Reggiano DOP.**

ORIGIN: Somerset, England

FLAVOUR NOTES: Umami, buttery, grassy

PAIRS WELL WITH: A Somerset Pomona apple liqueur, an apple-cider sangria, or a scrumpy cider

Cheddar

(Unpasteurised and Pasteurised, Cows' Milk, Traditional and Vegetarian Rennet)

Cheddar in one page. Yikes, that is a hefty challenge. Cheddar comes in so many varieties that it is impossible to generalise. When visiting your cheese shop or a big supermarket, try to taste the Cheddars and find the flavours you are accustomed to, or those you enjoy, and go from there. I have favourite Cheddars, but I will always taste the varieties, as each wheel and each batch are different.

There are two main distinctions of real Cheddar: farmhouse clothbound Cheddar and block Cheddar. It can be argued (I will argue this) that the clothbound cheeses are the only real, traditional cheddar. Clothbound Cheddars are large, 25kg+ truckles that are wrapped in muslin. This is integral to the characteristics of a clothbound Cheddar, and you will see, when they are in their maturing rooms, the cloth gets covered in the most beautiful collection of moulds, which impart flavours poles apart from block Cheddar. Block Cheddars are generally vacuum-packed immediately after production and matured in this way. This means that they are rindless – and once they are vacuum-sealed, there is no further influence from the outside world.

Although Cheddar is a name used all over the world, the cheese originates in the West Country of England, and this is true Cheddar. There are two you should seek out where you can. These are Montgomery's Cheddar, who are based in North Cadbury, Somerset, and Hafod, who are in . . . Wales!

In flavour, farmhouse clothbound Cheddar is wildly different from industrial block Cheddar. On the nose it is earthy, musty, grassy, rich and milky. On the palate, I could write an essay, but common flavours to come through are milk, grass, hay and spice. Block Cheddars have an aroma of warm, sweet milk, and on the palate, a sweetness, high acidity and cooked-dairy flavours.

Hard

If you like Cheddar, you'll also like many other types of Cheddar that are markedly different.

ORIGIN: Western Switzerland

FLAVOUR NOTES: Umami, brothy, vegetal

PAIRS WELL WITH: A spicy white wine like Jean-Louis Chave Sélection Circa or Junmai Daiginjo saké

Le Gruyère AOP

(Unpasteurised, Cows' Milk, Traditional Rennet)

When I worked in Borough Market, a well-established food market in London, we would sample out cheese to customers who may not have been there looking specifically for cheese. With thousands of customers walking through the market daily, you must give them something that they will remember. The cheese that I loved to do this with was Le Gruyère from the maturing house Huguenin Fromages.

The Gruyère region has been known for cheesemaking since the early twelfth century. The cheeses are available in different ages, plus Organic and Alpage forms. They are all enormous and weigh a minimum of 25kg – and they make for excellent gym equipment, which you can eat afterwards as a reward.

The cheese matured at Huguenin is multidimensional. It starts off milky, sweet and very pleasant. In the time it takes to walk away from a market stall, it develops and crescendos into something more complex, savoury, brothy and rich. Not every Gruyère is as rich as this, but they all have similar characteristics of umami, fruit and nuts.

Gruyère is such a versatile cheese, elevating any cheeseboard and a number of dishes, including soufflé and fondue.

Hard

If you like Le Gruyère AOP, you'll also like Comté AOP.

ORIGIN: Leicestershire, England

FLAVOUR NOTES: Savoury, grassy, milky

PAIRS WELL WITH: A full-bodied white wine, or a pumpkin ale like Brooklyn Brewery Post Road

Red Leicester

(Unpasteurised and Pasteurised, Cows' Milk, Traditional and Vegetarian Rennet)

One of my favourite comfort meals, which takes me back to being a child, is block Red Leicester cut into slices and grilled on toast. For real nostalgia it must be block Red Leicester and a generic white sliced loaf with slatherings of butter. I would always look forward to eating it after coming home from school and I still go to it now if I am feeling fragile or blue.

Red Leicester comes in both blocks and rounds. The block which you find readily in supermarkets is higher in its moisture content and with a texture which bends and snaps like a limp carrot. The flavour is simple, milky and kind. There are only a couple of producers today who make a traditional unpasteurised Red Leicester, and this includes the inimitable Sparkenhoe Red Leicester. This is a cheese that, along with all its prestige, also makes a cheese on toast of champions. I mostly like to eat it as it is, on a cheeseboard and as far away as possible from a sliced, bleached white loaf. The texture has a good snap to it and it has a deep orange hue in appearance. On the nose you will find some earthy notes from the rind and a mixture of fresh milk, nuts, and savoury, brothy elements. The palate is a continuation of the aroma, with a finishing mouthfeel of rich cream and dairy.

Hard

If you like Red Leicester, you'll also like Farmhouse Cheddar.

FLAVOUR
SWEET AND NUTTY

We all love a sweet and nutty cheese, but what do we mean by this? These are two flavour descriptors that we overuse in the cheese world. Perhaps because they are the easiest to identify and there are so many cheeses which broadly match the description. Many supermarket and deli labels use this terminology because we all know and love these flavours. Similar to being told, as an English Literature student, never to use the word 'nice', we as cheesemongers are time and time again told not to use 'sweet and nutty', but to find some more in-depth adjectives. Yes, it may be sweet, but what kind of sweet is it? Is it a fresh-fruit sweet or a confectionery sweet? What variety of nut are you tasting – the difference in flavour between a walnut and a pistachio is extreme. Can you really taste a nut? 'Sweet and nutty' is a very good base point, as you will see, with some of the most common cheeses sitting in this section. These flavours are inviting, comforting, easy eating, sessionable and complex in many ways. It is totally fine to pick up on sweet and nutty to start; it shows that you are developing and training your palate. The next stage is to think and analyse even further. Next time you are eating a piece of Comté, ask yourself: are you tasting Werther's Original sweets and macadamia or Strawberry Daquiri and Walnut? Remember, tasting is fun; try to relate flavours back to the memory bank in your head.

ORIGIN: Franche-Comté, France

FLAVOUR NOTES: Fruity, buttery, grassy

PAIRS WELL WITH: Wines like vin jaune and MacVin du Jura, or an amber beer like Pietra

Comté AOP

(Unpasteurised, Cows' Milk, Traditional Rennet)

Comté is a cheese that everyone likes. It has flavour profiles that we enjoy in cheese and many more foodstuffs. Comté comes from the Jura, where we see several larger mountain cheeses, loosely dubbed 'Alpines', produced. This means that the curd has been heated to a higher temperature than other cheeses and scalded to remove more moisture allowing for these large cheeses to mature and reach their full ageing potential without perishing. As we discussed in the beginning of this chapter, removing excess water is essential to making hard cheeses firstly, hard, and secondly, aged.

Comté cheesemaking has three distinct stages, which differentiates it from many other types of cheese. Having specialists at all three stages is integral to the quality of Comté:

1. The milking happens at numerous dairies.
2. The cheesemaking takes place at a *fruitière* (cheesemaking dairy) using the milk from Stage 1.
3. The cheeses are then looked after by affineurs who specialise in the maturing and development of Comté cheese.

Sweet and nutty are just two words to describe Comté cheese as a starting point and there are hundreds more – from grassy, to earthy, to mushroom, to sweat. I'm not so sure I like the latter, but it appears on the Comté flavour wheel. (I prefer 'saline'.) If you are just starting out in your cheese journey, Comté is one cheese I would recommend as a gateway into the beyond.

Hard

If you like Comté AOP, you'll also like Beaufort AOP.

ORIGIN: Nationwide, the Netherlands

FLAVOUR NOTES: Sweet, umami, butter

PAIRS WELL WITH: A Gamay like Armand Heitz Juliénas,
a strong ale, or a Dark & Stormy

Gouda

(Unpasteurised, Cows' Milk, Traditional Rennet)

The first cheese that anyone will mention when asked for a cheese from the Netherlands will no doubt be Gouda. It has a characteristic yellow rind, a squashed-sphere shape and the occasional hole dotted throughout.

Gouda is named after a town in Holland . . . called Gouda. Interestingly, it is not where Gouda was made but where it was distributed. This is because, in the Middle Ages, only certain municipalities were permitted to weigh and sell cheese. This is a tradition which continues to this day – you can head to Gouda on certain days at certain times of the year to see the cheeses displayed and ready for sale on the cobbled streets.

Gouda varies greatly in texture and flavour through different age profiles. The pliable texture of a young Gouda comes from a specific technique during the make process. Some hot water is added to the curds, which, in turn, dilutes the whey. In doing this you are removing some of the lactose from the curds, meaning there is less for the starter cultures to turn into lactic acid. Less acid results in a sweeter cheese. This process also removes some of the calcium, so instead of having a more brittle, firm texture, you find its characteristic rubbery, pliable texture instead.

Gouda comes in a whole variety of ages, but they all have a sweet, caramel, cooked flavour in common.

Hard

If you like Gouda, you'll also like Mimolette.

ORIGIN: Savoie, France

FLAVOUR NOTES: Sweet, grassy, savoury

PAIRS WELL WITH: A Pinot Noir like Phelps Creek Vineyards Cuvée Alexandrine, a dubbel beer, or a non-peated whisky

Beaufort AOP

(Unpasteurised, Cows' Milk, Traditional Rennet)

Beaufort is an enormous raw-milk hard cheese made in Eastern France with milk from Tarine and Abondance cows. Before Beaufort, there was a cheese named 'Grovire' made in the Beaufortain, Tarentaise and Maurienne valleys. It was a very popular cheese during the French Revolution and, in 1865, its name changed to 'Beaufort', after the Beaufortain valley.

I love Beaufort very much. It is so much more than just sweet and nutty. Beaufort is an Alpine cheese that sits in the same category as Comté and Gruyère and weighs in at a whopping 40kg.

Beaufort has a distinctive concave rind, which historically would have appeared from the strap placed around the cheese, to carry it down the mountain, but is now created with a wooden corset of sorts called a *'cercle à Beaufort'*.

Young Beaufort is wonderfully sweet, milky and with a little zippy acidity on occasion. As it ages on and matures, it develops a more rounded, grassy and complex flavour. If you can find a Beaufort Chalet d'Alpage where the cows have been grazing at a higher altitude (among other requirements), then grab it and don't let it go until you put it into your face.

Hard

If you like Beaufort AOP, you'll also like Comté AOP.

ORIGIN: Normandy, France

FLAVOUR NOTES: Caramel, savoury, salty

PAIRS WELL WITH: A full-bodied red wine like a
Malbec, or Trappist/abbey beers

Mimolette

(Unpasteurised or Pasteurised, Cows' Milk, Traditional Rennet)

Mimolette is a bright orange ball. The most excellent type of cheesy marketing, its colour and shape is distinctive. Mimolette is a cheese from northern France that looks like a cannon ball. It is orange due to the adding of annatto and round to mimic cheeses from the Netherlands such as Edam.

To add to these irregularities, it is covered in craters, giving an aesthetic of the Moon. These are intentional and are created by mites, little insects that are actively encouraged to take residence on the rind. Mites can be the bane of cheesemakers' lives where they pop up unwanted – for instance, in Cheddar ageing (perhaps the Cheddar makers should sell them to the Mimolette makers or make a Mimolette-style on the side!) – however, in Mimolette they are integral to its characteristics.

This cheese is an absolute pain to cut. Customers love it and mongers hate it. Mimolette has a very hard texture – especially with the Extra Vieille (extra old) cheeses. To open a Mimolette you need a university degree and a lot of muscle. It is simple in its flavour profile, with a sweet-caramel palate reminiscent of Gouda styles and a soy-sauce umami in the more aged cheeses.

Hard

If you like Mimolette, you'll also like aged Gouda.

ORIGIN: Bern, Switzerland

FLAVOUR NOTES: Sweet, nutty, fruity

PAIRS WELL WITH: A dry Riesling like Ansgar Clüsserath
Trittenheimer Apotheke, a Kölsch beer

Emmentaler AOP

(Unpasteurised, Cows' Milk, Traditional Rennet)

Emmentaler is THE cartoon cheese. It is the iconic depiction of a cheese in illustrative, describable, and now even emoji form.

Emmentaler is the most gargantuan of cheeses, weighing in from 70kg up to a whopping 120kg. Now, I have many a photo of me holding a whole cheese – Comté at 35kg, Beaufort at 42kg – but an Emmentaler would be the end of me.

It is a cheese originating from the Canton of Bern in Switzerland. It can sometimes be called 'Swiss' but this is a bit of a bastardisation of terms, as it can also refer to other cheeses that are imitations of this classic. Its iconic appearance is due to the big holes inside it, which we call 'eyes'. These eyes are made intentionally, and they are not the result of an old man sitting there carving holes, nor a mouse (sorry cartoons); they are created by gas production. A combination of propionic acid, acetic acid and carbon dioxide are produced during the fermentation process by the bacteria *Propionibacterium freudenreichii*. These not only create the holes, but also are integral to the flavour profile of this style of cheese.

Emmentaler has the most sweet and nutty flavour profile of them all. In addition, it exhibits fruity flavours – sometimes tropical fruit like pineapple – in the more aged cheeses.

Hard

If you like Emmentaler AOP, you will also like Jarlsberg.

Blue

Six

'I don't like blue cheese' is something I hear time and time again as a cheese-monger. Blue cheese can be daunting by merit of its appearance and the graphic illustration of eating mould, but if you think about it, all cheese is mould – it just isn't always blue.

Blue cheeses are, for the most part, those that have had blue moulds added into the milk. The desired strain of blue mould is added early in the production stage, lying dormant until later. Blue moulds need oxygen to grow, and this is why these cheeses are pierced. Large needles create pathways in the cheese, allowing the dormant moulds to react with oxygen. The amount of blue depends on the amount of piercing, so more channels will mean more oxygen, leading to more blue. The texture of the cheese greatly influences this also – a very compact blue cheese will only allow the blue to grow where the needles have pierced, whereas a softer, more open-textured cheese will allow the blues to form in the natural crevices also. There are a small number of blue cheeses that are not pierced and do not have blue moulds added into their milk. These are a rare and natural way of making blue cheeses, and I am delighted to introduce these to you in the final section in this chapter.

I strongly believe that there is a blue cheese for everyone. Like washed rinds, blue cheeses get a bad press and yet, as you will see throughout this chapter, they are not always over-powering. Some have minimal blue veins, and others have different strains of blue mould that aren't as strong.

'Strong blue cheese' is a term we all use; however, it doesn't really refer to anything. 'Strong' can have spicy notes, acidity, complex flavours – and, in some cases, using the word 'strong' can indicate that the cheese is past its best. With blues, 'strong' generally refers to the piquant, spicy notes dominant in cheeses such as Roquefort (page 160), but it is good to determine what you mean by strength so you can learn which cheeses are similar – or not. To do this, taste and calibrate with your local cheesemonger, or at home.

I have tried blue cheeses which, in a blind tasting, cannot be distinguished as blue. Even Blue Stilton (page 168) and Roquefort, which are known for being spicy beasts, can be very approachable. Each producer creates cheeses with slightly different techniques in making, piercing and ageing, and because of this, the same cheeses from multiple producers can be more mellow, fruity, yeasty and buttery. My favourite blue cheese, Stichelton (page 166), is not pierced until it has aged for approximately six weeks, so the flavours of the cheese itself are able to blossom, develop and hold their own before the blue mould moves in and leaves its clothes everywhere and its toothbrush in the bathroom. Blues are not always painful; they have some beautiful flavour nuances throughout. A lot of this is down to the skill of the cheesemaker in making delicious cheese, even prior to the blueing taking hold. This, plus the skill of making sure that there is a balance of flavours and not just a punch in the face.

If you are not sure about blue cheeses, but you are a 'try everything once' person, then I strongly recommend tasting a few with your local cheesemonger. They will know how all the cheeses are tasting at that moment and can make recommendations. Cheesemongers are generally not sadistic (I can't vouch for everyone), so if you say you want to try a mild blue, they will find you a mild blue. Another tip is to try the cheeses very cold. Just as wines are restrained and muted when chilled too much, so is cheese. This makes for an excellent chilled snack on a summer afternoon or a gateway introduction into the realms of the spicy blue.

Blue cheeses can be texturally soft, semi-hard or hard. They generally sit in the soft and semi-hard sections, as this texture and moisture content allows for the blue moulds to grow more effectively. Moulds like damp conditions and thrive better this way. In this chapter we will analyse the flavours of blue cheese a little more, to hopefully match make you with a blue you perhaps wouldn't have thought to eat before.

FLAVOUR
PIQUANT

Piquant is a feeling more than a simple flavour. It is a sensation that is felt in the mouth, especially on the tongue, and it is frequently associated with foods whose flavours give this feeling. Spicy Asian cuisine, mustard and even black pepper are flavour associates to this sensation. I personally associate spice with pain, as I have a very low threshold. Certain foods can trigger the perception of heat even when it is not there. Although chilli is not hot in temperature, it stimulates the same pain receptors, which are free nerve endings in the oral mucosa. This is the same with foods like strong blue cheese, pepper, garlic and mint. When you eat these foods, the pain receptors are stimulated, and they send signals via the trigeminal nerve to the brain. The cranial nerves are responsible for taste. When we eat strong blue cheeses like Roquefort (page 160), we can taste pepper from the blue moulds, but we are also experiencing a reaction in our mouths that gives the sensation of heat. I have tasted some blue cheeses that have this in such excess that it almost feels painful and eventually numbing, like an anaesthetic. This, along with the intense umami, is perhaps why we do not all like to eat strong blue cheeses and why, if we do, we do not always want to eat too much of them. The cheeses in this section give both a spicy feeling in the mouth as well as characteristic peppery flavours.

Blue

ORIGIN: Aveyron, France

FLAVOUR NOTES: Piquant, buttery, fruity

PAIRS WELL WITH: A sweet Loire white wine like a
Bonnezeaux Château de Fesles,
a Baltic porter, or Armagnac

Roquefort AOP

(Unpasteurised, Ewes' Milk, Traditional Rennet)

I will not entertain the stories of lovers in caves and forgotten sandwiches in this book – you can look up the stories and myths about Roquefort elsewhere if you are looking for a giggle. Here, we are looking at flavour, darling. Roquefort is known for being super strong and is certainly not a starting point for those who dislike blues. I will always say, 'Try something once', but I completely understand that it is a concentrated bomb of flavour and spice, so it may not be for the cheese fainthearted.

I will, however, say this. Roquefort is made seasonally. Therefore, adjustments must be made to the cheese to allow for year-round production, owing to the demand of Roquefort fans. At certain times of the year, the cheeses will be younger and at other times, older, so it doesn't always taste the same or have the same level of intensity. A top tip for summer blue-cheese eating is to eat it straight out of the fridge. We know that fridge temperatures somewhat mute the flavours of food and alcohol, so a Roquefort choc-ice may be the breakthrough method in finding your newfound love for Roquefort. A good Roquefort has much more to it than a kick in your face. It has a buttery, salty flavour that melts in your mouth, with flavours of fruit and alcohol heavily seasoning it.

Blue

If you like Roquefort AOP, you'll also like Lanark Blue.

ORIGIN: Asturias, Spain

FLAVOUR NOTES: Spicy, tropical, bitter

PAIRS WELL WITH: A full-bodied Zinfandel, a medium-dry sherry like Barbadillo Amontillado Medium Dry Sherry, or Spanish sidra (cider)

Cabrales DOP

(Unpasteurised, Cows' milk or a mixture of cow, goat and ewe milk, Traditional Rennet)

If you have tried Cabrales, you will know about it. There is no 'Hmm, maybe I have tried it, I can't quite remember.' It is black and white, like tasting the infamously foul-tasting Greenland shark. Unlike Greenland shark, which should be banished from the plates of the earth, Cabrales is a tasty cheese. I know I have said that 'strong' is not a great adjective for describing cheese, but I will wholeheartedly allow it when it comes to Cabrales, as it is strong in every sense.

This is a blue cheese matured in caves in Asturias in Spain. It is THE strongest blue cheese I have ever tried, bar none. There are many producers of Cabrales and the flavours and textures in cheeses made by these cheesemakers can vary hugely. Cabrales does a strange thing – when we think of cheeses getting older, we think of them getting stronger, more complex, more concentrated in flavour, and not the reverse. Cabrales does the reverse. The ageing process somewhat mellows the cheese and allows for a delightfully creamy texture to develop, and flavours of mango and other tropical fruits come out alongside the potent spice. It may make a grown adult cry outside of Spain, but here, strong blues are incredibly popular, and, well, children in Asturias eat Cabrales sandwiches in their school break, so . . .

Blue

If you like Cabrales DOP, you'll also like very, very spicy things.

ORIGIN: Lanarkshire, Scotland

FLAVOUR NOTES: Spicy, creamy, animal

PAIRS WELL WITH: Sauternes sweet wine, Islay whisky, or blueberry juice

Lanark Blue

(Unpasteurised, Ewes' Milk, Traditional Rennet)

Lanark Blue is a strong, spicy blue from Lanarkshire in Scotland. It is made by Errington Cheese, a family cheesemaker which first started up in the early 1980s. It is made using the milk of Lacaune ewes, the same breed used to make Roquefort (page 160) and St James (page 74). Errington Cheese also make cows'-milk cheeses, collecting milk from a neighbouring farm, and in recent years, they purchased a herd of dairy goats to start making lactic cheeses.

Lanark Blue is made seasonally, as the milking takes place between the months of January to September. Because of this you will see slight fluctuations in age profiles of these cheeses outside of the season when milk is not being produced. It is a powerful blue with a heady aroma of cereal, alcohol, ammonia and animal. On the palate, the texture is fudgy but giving, with the occasional crunch from the moulds within. The palate here is as powerful as the nose. It is spicy and peppery with a buttery cereal undertone. This one is not for the fainthearted.

Blue

If you like Lanark Blue, you'll also like Roquefort AOP.

ORIGIN: Vermont, USA

FLAVOUR NOTES: Spicy, mushroom, aromatic

PAIRS WELL WITH: A sparkling Shiraz like Peter Lehmann
Black Queen, a stout beer, or black coffee

Bayley Hazen Blue

(Unpasteurised, Cows' Milk, Traditional Rennet)

American cheeses receive a lot of criticism, but I assure you they are not just plastic slices and Velveeta. There are some outstanding artisanal cheeses across the country, and Jasper Hill Farm, who make Bayley Hazen Blue, and many others, are at the forefront. Their Bayley Hazen Blue is a blue cheese which is cylindrical in format, like the Fourme D'Ambert (page 174) and Fourme de Montbrison (page 167) from France.

Jasper Hill Farm are not only experts in cheesemaking, but they also have an extensive underground cave-ageing system to mature their cheeses. Maturing and affinage is what takes a cheese from good to great.

Bayley Hazen Blue has a dense and fudge-like texture, and the combination of raw milk and cheesemaking expertise at Jasper Hill give it great complexity. The aromas are yeasty, sweet and mushroomy. On the palate, a refined sweetness comes through from the milk and the breakdown within the cheese. There is a fabulous spice – think aniseed and pepper – which is balanced nicely by the characteristics of the milk – grass, hay and a nutty finish.

Blue

If you like Bayley Hazen Blue, you'll also like
Fourme de Montbrison AOP.

ORIGIN: Oregon, USA

FLAVOUR NOTES: Piquant, fruity, boozy

PAIRS WELL WITH: A late-harvest Riesling like a Beerenauslese from Germany, a barley wine, or a Poire Williams eau de vie

Rogue River Blue

(Unpasteurised, Cows' Milk, Traditional Rennet)

Rogue River Blue is perhaps the most visually iconic cheese from the USA. Its appearance is beautiful and unmistakeable. This is one of the first American cheeses that I learned about, as I was lucky enough to sell it in Whole Foods Market, where I worked early in my cheese career. It is a blue cheese which has won numerous awards, including Supreme Champion twice at the World Cheese Awards.

Rogue River Blue is made seasonally and biodynamically, with its release falling in November each year. Owing to its production methods, artisanal guise and having to travel from Oregon, it comes out in the UK at a cost of about 47 million pounds a kilo, so it is most certainly one to savour when you find it.

This blue is beautifully presented, with an ivory paste, generous blue-green veining and wrapped in vine leaves. The leaves are macerated in a pear brandy, which, in turn, gives it a very fruity, boozy flavour and a creamy palate. Luckily, the flavours are concentrated, complex and rich, so you do not have to eat too much of it to appreciate it. One of the reasons for its complexity comes from the ageing of the cheese. Before it is released, it is aged between 9 and 11 months to allow the cheese to fully develop and for the flavours to relax and mature.

Blue

If you like Rogue River Blue, you'll also like Basajo.

FLAVOUR
MALT

I recently went up to Edinburgh to train some cheesemongers on how to enhance their retail skills. As well as eating a lot of cheese, part of my job involves teaching others how to work with it and love it as much as I do. I love walking around Edinburgh and always find myself meandering for hours on end, when if I was at home, I would moan and get a taxi instead of walking. There is so much to see, hear and smell. When walking to my hotel, I could smell bread. It was an odd time to be smelling fresh bread being baked (in the evening), but I went with it and enjoyed the addition to my sensory experience. On the morning of the class, we opened a blue cheese to taste with the group, and the smell was identical. The aroma around Edinburgh was in fact malt, and the cheese transported me straight back to 12 hours prior and walking through the Old Town. Malty flavours in cheese are fabulous and they make for excellent cheeses to pair. These cheeses sometimes showcase characteristics of cereal, biscuit and toasted grain, and they go incredibly well with beers, stouts and even sherry and spirits. As malt's characteristics can show toasty flavours and dried nuts, these cheeses are a great match with sweet wines.

Blue

ORIGIN: Nottinghamshire, England

FLAVOUR NOTES: Yeast, savoury, fruit

PAIRS WELL WITH: A sweet white wine like De Bortoli Noble
One Botrytis Sémillon, a Scotch ale or Islay whisky

Stichelton

(Unpasteurised, Cows' Milk, Traditional Rennet)

Stichelton is one of my favourite cheeses, made by one of my favourite people. This makes it taste even more delicious. Fact. It is a raw-milk blue cheese made by Joe Schneider and his team in Nottinghamshire. Stichelton is a cheese that never fails to grace my Christmas table, and most other tables, throughout the year. On Collingthwaite Farm on the Welbeck Estate, using milk from their herd of cows a stone's throw away (please don't throw stones at the cows), Joe transforms the milk into 8kg truckles of sheer excellence daily.

Until 1992 Stilton was permitted to be made with both unpasteurised and pasteurised milk. Stichelton is the brainchild of Joe, and Randolph Hodgson, who wanted to make sure that this historical make was not lost in time, even if it cannot be called Stilton. The recipe shows very little intervention, with minimal amounts of starters and rennet added into the milk. The cheese is most certainly an expression of Joe's understanding of the raw milk and how to influence its ever-changing temperament.

Stichelton has a characteristic orange-red hue to its rind, and an ivory paste, which is not necessarily packed with blue veins. The cheeses are allowed to ripen before being pierced, which develops the flavour profile of the cheese itself and not just the blueing. As it is a raw-milk cheese, there are many factors that affect its flavour. The season is just one of these factors, but a considerable one. In late summer and autumn, the flavours are more caramel and sweet, whereas the winter cheeses exhibit more flavours of malt, stock and meat. Stichelton always has a creamy undertone and a gentle spice.

Blue

If you like Stichelton, you're a friend of mine.

ORIGIN: Haut-Forez, France

FLAVOUR NOTES: Malty, fermented, spicy

PAIRS WELL WITH: An oaked Chardonnay, a white port like Churchill's, or a pale ale

Fourme de Montbrison AOP

(Unpasteurised, Cows' Milk, Traditional Rennet)

Fourme de Montbrison is a cheese hailing from the Haut-Forez in France. It is a blue cheese, similar in form (*fourme*) to the more widely known Fourme D'Ambert (page 174), yet with a distinctive character. Unlike many French blue cheeses, it has a much firmer and drier paste thanks to its production method. Stages within its make even appear reminiscent of Cheddar production, with curds knitting together and being stacked before milling and salting. The following stages are quite beautiful. The cylinders are taken out of their moulds. Where cheeses like Cheddar and Comté are matured on wooden boards, Fourme de Montbrison is matured in concave, wooden gutter-like boards made from spruce. For six days the cheeses are turned a quarter turn every two hours – and here is where they begin to take on their characteristic orange rind. Despite the appearance, the cheeses are never washed, only turned. They are then matured in caves for a minimum of three weeks. I was fortunate enough to visit a maturing cave for the cheeses at Fromagerie des Hautes Chaumes, where a working water mill is used to create the caves' humidity.

The cheeses have a characteristic yeasty and almost woody flavour to them. There is a lot of variation between the cheeses from different producers, but I particularly enjoy those from Fromagerie des Hautes Chaumes, in which there is an excellent mix of spice, malt, alcohol, fruit and dairy.

Blue

If you like Fourme de Montbrison AOP, you'll also like Stichelton.

ORIGIN: Nottinghamshire, Leicestershire or Derbyshire, England

FLAVOUR NOTES: Malty, buttery, fruity

PAIRS WELL WITH: A tawny port, a porter beer, or VSOP Cognac

Blue Stilton PDO

(Pasteurised, Cows' Milk, Vegetarian Rennet)

Stilton is a household name in the cheese world. Blue Stilton is the most common, but its sibling White Stilton also owns a PDO (Protected Designation of Origin) status. Blue Stilton is made by six dairies throughout the counties of Nottinghamshire, Leicestershire and Derbyshire. It must be made with pasteurised milk.

Stilton is known to be a strong cheese, but it really is much more than that. In fact, the best are not very strong. They are more balanced with flavours from the cheese itself, and not just from the blue moulds. Stilton is a crumbly cheese, and its make is slow. The cheeses are not pierced immediately, so the flavours of the cheese are allowed to develop before the blue moulds take hold. This gives a more complex yet balanced flavour, whereby you can taste more of the milk itself. The texture is crumbly yet giving. When biting into a piece of Stilton, you can leave teeth marks as if it were a soft fudge. Stilton is yeasty, spicy, buttery, savoury and fruity.

Vegetarians should note that as well as making Stilton with vegetarian rennet, Colston Bassett Creamery makes a Blue Stilton exclusively for Neal's Yard Dairy which uses animal rennet. The texture is even more yielding. One to seek out!

Blue

If you like Blue Stilton PDO, you'll love Stichelton.

ORIGIN: Northern England

FLAVOUR NOTES: Fruity, yeasty, salty

PAIRS WELL WITH: A Vin Santo dessert wine, a barley wine, or nocino walnut liqueur

Shropshire Blue

(Unpasteurised, Cows' Milk, Traditional Rennet)

Shropshire Blue is a vibrant-orange-coloured blue cheese. The origins of this cheese aren't completely clear, but it is clear that despite the misleading name, the cheese isn't believed to have a connection to Shropshire. The cheese is currently made in Nottinghamshire and Leicestershire. It is a British cheese recipe with the addition of annatto to make it orange. This is why you will see several Stilton cheesemakers also making a Shropshire Blue. The annatto provides more than just the colouring. In the form used for cheesemaking, it is alkaline. This means that it raises the pH of milk very slightly when it is added in. Because of this, and the higher pH at the time rennet is added, it takes longer to harden, which results in a higher moisture cheese. For this reason, you will find that Shropshire Blue is a little softer in texture than a Stilton. In aroma, it is yeasty and fruity. On the palate, the yeast pursues and continues, the mouthfeel is soft and fudgy, and the flavours are yeasty, fruity, spicy and a little bitter at the end.

Blue

If you like Shropshire Blue, you'll also like Blue Stilton PDO.

FLAVOUR
FRUIT

As I have mentioned, I am a firm believer that there is a blue cheese for everyone. In the Piquant section (pages 159–64) we concentrated on powerful, complex and intense-flavoured blues, but here, we are looking at those which are more approachable. Not all blues want to punch you in the face, and some of these can be considered 'lighter' and even 'gateway' blues. These are blue cheeses with either minimal blueing, or their blue is gentle and balanced by other flavours. I have blind-tasted one of these cheeses with customers who were unable to identify that the cheese was even blue. Flavour and taste are a lot about perception, and when you are staring a mouldy piece of food in the face, your instinct and primal sensors are going to give you a warning. These cheeses are supple, creamy, gentle, and buttery, with small pockets of blue throughout. Some of these use strains of *Penicillium* which are gentler than the *Penicillium Roqueforti* found in the Piquant section. If you are not a blue fan or are new to cheese and want to work yourself in slowly with blue cheeses, this is where to start. The flavours are simpler, gentler and more rounded – and will not bite, I promise.

ORIGIN: Lombardy and Piedmont, Italy

FLAVOUR NOTES: Fruity, yeasty, yogurty

PAIRS WELL WITH: A sparkling white wine like Moscato d'Asti,
a fruit beer, or a Spiced Rum Daiquiri

Gorgonzola Dolce DOP

(Unpasteurised, Cows' Milk, Traditional Rennet)

I used to sell this cheese in a grocery store, where we would cut the top off and scoop out the insides. It's a delicious way of eating it, but perhaps less appealing when looking at food waste. Interestingly, the regulatory body for Gorgonzola DOP does say not to eat the rind of this cheese, but I still do! In this grocery store, I always said on my last day that I would plant my face in the bowl. Fortunately for the shop, I did not do this, but the urge was strong.

The most indulgent thing I have done with this cheese was with an old boss, and we 'truffled' a wheel. The first attempt was in a walk-in freezer with a table, wires and a wheel of cheese. With us in our white coats, it really looked like something out of a horror film. The second time we removed the entire contents of the cheese from the rind, mixed it with truffle and mascarpone and popped it back in. This was both successful and tasty.

Gorgonzola Dolce is a very soft, creamy and indulgent blue cheese. It can be simple, sweet and light in its blueing, but it can also have a lot more spice than expected.

Blue

If you like Gorgonzola Dolce DOP, you'll also like Beauvale.

ORIGIN: Bavaria, Germany

FLAVOUR NOTES: Creamy, fruity, yeasty

PAIRS WELL WITH: Orange wines from Friuli,
or a Jurançon Moelleux dessert wine

Montagnolo Affine

(Pasteurised, Cows' Milk, Vegetarian Coagulant)

Montagnolo Affine is a cheese that sounds remarkably Italian for a German cheese. It is the sister cheese of Cambozola, which is also made by Käserei Champignon in Bavaria.

As with many of the enhanced cheeses in the Bloomy Rind chapter, the milk for this cheese has been enhanced with cream. This is a blue cheese for those who are hesitant with their love for blue or are at the beginning of their blue journey. Blind, this could be a triple cream alone, as the blue is very restrained. To develop its characteristic texture and flavour profile, it undergoes a slow and cold maturation process, which allows the cheese to develop and not to be overpowered by the blueing.

The cheese has been very successful in cheese competitions, having taken the Supreme Champion prize in both the World Cheese Awards and the International Cheese Awards. It continues to be a success and is now more widely distributed because of its popularity. The resulting paste is rich, creamy and a little sour. The texture softens and coats the mouth, and flavours are fruity, creamy and clean. There are also biscuity, yeasty and savoury notes within.

Blue

If you like Montagnolo Affine, you'll also like Brillat-Savarin IGP.

ORIGIN: Leeds, England

FLAVOUR NOTES: Fruity, buttery, biscuity

PAIRS WELL WITH: A sweet wine such as Recioto di Soave, or a sweet cider

Leeds Blue

(Pasteurised, Ewes' Milk, Traditional Rennet)

Leeds Blue is a pasteurised cheese that proves that pasteurisation can still lead to great things. Yes, pasteurisation removes a lot of the natural flora within milk. However, tasting Leeds Blue and its batch variation makes you realise how much skill is still involved from the cheesemaker, how the hand manipulation is very important and how not every cheese tastes the same.

Leeds Blue is made by Mario Olianas up in the north of England. Sardinian by birth, Mario started his cheesemaking journey in his kitchen in 2012 and is now supplying his cheeses to some of the best cheesemongers, distributors and restaurants in the UK. He collects his milk from the local area and transforms it into this cheese and a host of others, including some excellent Pecorino-style cheeses.

Leeds Blue (also known as Yorkshire Pecorino Blue) is a continental-style blue cheese. It has a great soft and giving texture, with a butteriness that melts in your mouth. The large pockets of blue are deceiving – the cheese is very approachable. The blueing is not too spicy, and the cheese is buttery, fruity, sweet and with a touch of a tang from the ewes' milk.

Blue

If you like Leeds Blue, you'll also like Fourme D'Ambert AOP.

ORIGIN: Auvergne, France

FLAVOUR NOTES: Yeast, mushroom, fruity

PAIRS WELL WITH: A sweet white wine like a
Tokaji Aszú 5 Puttonyos, an imperial stout, or cherry juice

Fourme D'Ambert AOP

(Unpasteurised, Cows' Milk, Traditional Rennet)

There is a church in the Auvergne, Église de la Chaulme, which has tithe stones with carvings depicting local regional products, including Fourme D'Ambert. This church was constructed in the Middle Ages, showing Fourme D'Ambert to have a long history. It also shows how cool the French are for carving cheese into their buildings.

Fourme D'Ambert is cylindrical in shape, with a height approximately double its width, giving a very distinguishable shape (known as a *'fourme'*) on a cheese counter. This cheese is now made in dairies and creameries, but in the past it was made in *'jasseries'*, a type of chalet around the region of Haut-Forez in the Loire Valley.

While some blues have veins, Fourme D'Ambert has pockets. These large, bubble-like crevices provide a different aesthetic than that of other blue cheeses. Although it appears to be very blue in colour and distribution, it is a mild cheese. The aroma is unmistakeably of mushroom, and when the rind is tacky and pink, there are yeasty notes and a washed-rind feel. The texture is fudgy and dense, with overall flavours of mushroom, gentle spice and butter.

Blue

If you like Fourme D'Ambert AOP, you'll also like
Fourme de Montbrison AOP.

ORIGIN: Tipperary, Ireland

FLAVOUR NOTES: Fruity, milky, biscuity

PAIRS WELL WITH: Prosecco, sloe gin, or rooibos tea

Cashel Blue

(Pasteurised, Cows' Milk, Vegetarian Rennet)

Cashel Blue is a cheese that has been made on the same farm in Tipperary since the early 1980s. It is named after the Rock of Cashel, a local historical site. The milk that they use to make the cheese comes from their own dairy herd, with the remainder collected from a 25km radius of the dairy, from pasture-fed herds.

Cashel Blue has a buttery, yeasty flavour profile with a lot of fruit, a mouth-watering acidity, milky notes and a gentle spice. It can age for approximately six months before it starts evolving into a spicy beast.

It comes in a very monger-friendly size and shape, and is nice to handle in its small stature and foil coating. Cashel Blue has a creamy yet fudgy paste with gentle blue veins throughout. This blue lends itself very well to cuisine, with many an appealing recipe creation already out in the world. I particularly enjoy the combination of Cashel Blue with pears and black pudding, and it also makes a great accompaniment to roasted figs.

Blue

If you like Cashel Blue, you'll also like Fourme D'Ambert AOP.

FLAVOUR
HERBACEOUS

I wanted to call this section 'Bitter', as there are some beautiful bitter flavours which you can find in blue cheeses, but there are many negative connotations of bitter, and I decided that these cheeses are much more than this. These are cheeses which have a sense of place (like the Animal section on pages 127–33) but this time, along with the milk and the animal, there is a lot more flavour information about the surroundings, the vegetation and the unique maturation environments. You most certainly cannot taste every blade of grass and plant that the animals have eaten, but there is an evident link.

The cheese Bleu de Termignon (page 177), for example, is a wild blue which has a different flavour profile each season – and even within each batch and wheel. One year I tasted cheeses that were fennel-like, another year bitter chicory, and flavours of vegetables, artichokes, mushroom and even cheese puffs in between. There is a distinct bitterness that can come through in many of these cheeses, and it is wholly welcome and not out of place. The bitter is a vegetal, and not a chemical, bitter and it speaks of the pasture and even the wild and natural production methods. These cheeses are all aged in caves and none of them have had blue moulds added into the milk, nor have they been pierced. The flavours of cave, earth and mushroom which come out in these cheeses are entirely natural, influenced and directly colonised by the microbes in the cave environment, giving them a flavour profile specific to their location.

ORIGIN: Savoie, France

FLAVOUR NOTES: Bitter, aniseed, wild

PAIRS WELL WITH: A Monbazillac sweet wine, a mead, or a Last Word cocktail

Bleu de Termignon

(Unpasteurised, Cows' Milk, Traditional Rennet)

Let's recall Salers from the Hard Cheese chapter (page 128) – a cheese which is every Environmental Health Officer's nightmare incarnate. Bleu de Termignon is another member of this tasty club. In the Blue Cheese chapter introduction, we talked about natural blues that have not been pierced, and this is one of them. There are no holes created in the cheese for the blue to grow in, just the natural crevices between the curd, which give pathways for the blue to take hold. Nor have the cheeses been inoculated with a blue mould at the beginning of their make; the blueing is entirely natural. As with all natural products – natural wines, natural anything – there is a huge amount of diversity, and these cheeses do not follow the rules. Each wheel can taste different, and this is what makes them so exciting. When the cheeses first come down from the mountain, they have minimal blueing and can taste very much like a British territorial cheese (e.g. Cheshire) with a prominent, zingy acidity. They can also taste like cheese puffs. As they age, wonderful flavours of chicory, artichoke, mushroom and aniseed come through, which are incredibly delicious.

This may sound like sacrilege, but I have eaten Bleu de Termignon crumbled over chips. It makes an excellent seasoning.

Blue

If you like Bleu de Termignon, you'll also like Castelmagno DOP.

ORIGIN: Piedmont, Italy

FLAVOUR NOTES: Bitter, herbal, yeasty

PAIRS WELL WITH: A Recioto della Valpolicella, or an Italian vermouth like Luigi Vico Vermouth di Torino

Castelmagno DOP

(Unpasteurised, Cows' Milk, Traditional Rennet)

There is a cheese festival organised by the Slow Food organisation every other year in a town called Bra, in Piedmont, Italy. This is one of the highlights of the cheese calendar for cheese lovers and professionals across the globe. It also happens to be the home of Castelmagno, a rare cheese that doesn't travel so widely. When I head to Piedmont, I stock up and I also order it from EVERY menu, as it works so well in food.

It is another cheese that has not been pierced nor inoculated. Castelmagno di Alpeggio is a mountain version of this cheese, which bears a Slow Food Presidium recognition. A Slow Food Presidia protects quality products at risk of extinction.

There are only a small handful of producers who make the cheese in this way, with raw milk, natural starters, and only in the summer months. One of the producers boasts a quantity of around 400 different species of herbs and plants found in the pasture eaten by the cows whose milk is used to make this special, complex and biodiverse cheese.

Castelmagno's flavours are mineral, salty and sour when young and as it develops you will find more vegetal, herbal and brothy, meaty notes developing. Castelmagno has similarities to Bleu de Termignon (page 177) in being a natural blue with some wild flavour profiles. Castelmagno's flavours perfectly complement dishes in Piedmont involving polenta and gnocchi.

Blue

If you like Castelmagno DOP, you'll also like Gamonéu DOP.

ORIGIN: Asturias, Spain

FLAVOUR NOTES: Herbal, smoked, earthy

PAIRS WELL WITH: A Spanish vermouth like the Vermut Xalar
from Coca i Fito, a scrumpy cider, or an apple juice

Gamonéu DOP

(Unpasteurised, Cows', Ewes' or Goats' Milk, Traditional Rennet)

Gamonéu is a wild cheese made in two villages in Asturias, Spain called Onís and Cangas de Onís. It is a raw-milk cheese which is smoked and then matured in caves, where it takes on its natural blueing. Like Bleu de Termignon (page 177) and Castelmagno (page 178), it is not pierced, nor is it inoculated with blue moulds.

There are two types: Gamonéu del Puerto and Gamonéu del Valle. Gamonéu del Puerto is produced seasonally, only in the spring and summer, and at a high altitude, with the cows on the complex, rich pasture. The cheeses are smoked over wood in the mountainous region of Asturias. Flavours are herbal, bitter, grassy, earthy, and mushroom. The smoking of the cheese using wood from local fruit trees adds an extra dimension.

Blue

If you like Gamonéu DOP, you'll also like Bleu de Termignon.

How to Create the
Perfect Cheeseboard

Now that you know how to taste cheese, you might well want to share your expertise with friends and family. It's most likely that you'll then need to put together a cheeseboard . . .

First off, my biggest piece of advice when putting together a cheeseboard for guests is to make sure you are choosing cheeses you like. If you don't like cheese at all, then get someone else to put it together.

Next, odd numbers are recommended. Create a board of three, five or seven cheeses. You cannot go wrong with a hard, soft (this is generally a bloomy rind, but can also come from the fresh or washed-rind categories too) and blue combination for variety. The reason why odd numbers are good is that they allow for adequate spacing and create a good aesthetic on a board. This usually ends up at a cheeseboard of about 67 cheeses for me, so think about the size of the board or plate that you will be presenting them on.

I generally choose a selection based on what is seasonal, what suits the occasion and what the cheesemongers are recommending. When you buy cheese, you want to eat it quickly, when it is at its best. Seasonality is my favourite focus when creating a cheeseboard. Cheeses are seasonal. Not all cheeses are made year-round. Goats and ewes kid and lamb annually in nature, and they have a shorter season than cows. It's worth noting that milk comes after calving/kidding/lambing, so we see an influx of goats'- and ewes'-milk cheeses in the spring. The cheese Mont D'Or (page 80) is also seasonal, as it is made in the autumn, when the cows come down from their high summer grazing and the milk composition is more suited to a soft cheese make.

Choosing cheese by season might be a bit overwhelming to begin with, so I have put together some examples of cheeseboards and themes that you can use for inspiration when creating your own. To give you guidance, they are all numbered in the order in which I would recommend eating them, from simpler flavours to more complex. All of these cheeses can be found in the pages of this book.

TRADITIONAL   The most classic cheeseboard consists of the bloomy rind, hard cheese and blue trifecta. I have chosen a royal threesome for this board. Brie de Meaux, the ultimate bloomy rind; my favourite traditional Cheddar, made by Jamie Montgomery; and the king of French blues, Roquefort.

1. Brie de Meaux AOP (France) (page 48)
2. Montgomery's Cheddar (England) (page 144)
3. Roquefort AOP (France) (page 160)

WEEKDAY   It's Wednesday, it's hump day and it is the wrong side of payday. These cheeses are widely available and make an excellent cheesy snack for any weeknight occasion. Pair these with some crackers and whatever chutney or jam you may have in the cupboard, and you are set!

1. Caprice des Dieux (France) (page 50)
2. Red Leicester (England) (page 146)
3. Cashel Blue (Ireland) (page 175)

FESTIVE   We put ourselves under a lot of pressure when curating the perfect festive cheeseboard. Looking back over my cheeseboards for the past six Christmases, I can see that I am actually a creature of habit. Below, you can see my favourite festive cheeseboard picks.

1. Crottin de Chavignol AOP (France) (page 36)
2. Coulommiers (France) (page 55)
3. Saint-Nectaire AOP (France) (page 99)
4. Torta de Barros (Spain) (page 73)
5. Beaufort AOP (France) (page 150)
6. Stichelton (England) (page 166)
7. Munster AOP (France) (page 93)

The Perfect Cheeseboard

EXPLORE AROUND THE WORLD   This selection covers cheeses from both new- and old-world regions. Remember to taste in the order written – you must always taste Cabrales last, as it will probably remove your taste buds for about four days . . .

1. Quesillo (Mexico) (page 21)
2. La Tur (Italy) (page 59)
3. Fromage de Herve AOP (Belgium) (page 85)
4. Raclette du Valais AOP (Switzerland) (page 92)
5. Cabrales DOP (Spain) (page 161)

CELEBRATE THE BRITISH ISLES   I will be curating this cheeseboard at the next possible occasion. Here, you will see a mixture of cheeses that have a continental influence or are a twist on a classic. The variety of colours, shapes and flavours in this selection makes the most stunning and delicious of cheeseboards.

1. St Jude (England) (page 39)
2. Tunworth (England) (page 54)
3. Celtic Promise (Wales) (page 75)
4. Carraignamuc (Ireland) (page 101)
5. Anster (Scotland) (page 110)
6. Lincolnshire Poacher (England) (page 138)
7. Blue Stilton PDO (England) (page 168)

THANKSGIVING   I am so excited about the American cheese scene now. As cheesemaker Joe Schneider says in the book *Cheese Champions*, 'A new generation of American cheesemakers have travelled the world in search of knowledge and inspiration and have brought back what they have learned.' There are some absolutely stunning cheeses out there and for this, I have put together an all-American cheeseboard for Thanksgiving, or any other celebration for that matter!

The Perfect Cheeseboard

1. Humboldt Fog (page 63)
2. Cornerstone (page 103)
3. Rush Creek Reserve (page 86)
4. Bayley Hazen Blue (page 163)
5. Dunbarton Blue (page 133)

GERMAN GREATS This board consists of three cheeses that have only been in existence for the last 40 years – with the Urstromshire taking its place as the newest recipe in the entire book, coming into existence only within the last few years. These are all incredibly exciting cheeses spanning different styles, from classics to newly created hybrids.

1. Grisette (page 41)
2. Urstromshire (page 109)
3. Deichkäse (page 140)

ITALIAN ICONS This is a stellar cheeseboard covering some iconic Italian cheeses from up and down the country. This board boasts five wholly different cheesemaking techniques and flavour profiles to give a snapshot of just a few of the amazing cheeses made in Italy.

1. La Tur (page 59)
2. Scamorza Affumicata (page 119)
3. Taleggio DOP (page 79)
4. Parmigiano Reggiano DOP (page 142)
5. Gorgonzola Dolce DOP (page 171)

FRENCH FAVOURITES I love French cheese so much that I could create an infinite number of cheeseboards and they would all work. Here, I have put together a cheese from each chapter, plus a cheeky seventh cheese to keep the numbers odd, as mentioned in my intro!

A Final (Tasting) Note

I am now very hungry after writing about all of these delicious cheeses.

My ultimate goal for this book is to get you all eating more cheese – more of the cheeses you love, with a firmer understanding of why you love them, as well as the desire to leave your comfort zone and try new things. Ideally, this comfort zone will have increased in size, or perhaps your zone boundaries have completely dissolved!

In the introduction I mentioned cheeses which are close to extinction. Not everything can be saved, unfortunately, but it would be a colossal shame if you didn't get to try these before they leave us, so I urge you to seek these out and taste them where you can. On the other side, I have mentioned cheeses which have just come into existence. Seek these out too, and give them some support at the beginning of their journey. I find it fascinating to watch a cheese develop and find its feet early on. New cheeses sometimes adjust their recipes in the beginning so that is a wonderful thing that we have the privilege to watch and taste as the recipe develops in real time. Now, for those classics. The classic cheeses in this book, the cheeses we all know and love, still need our loyalty. Yes, the shiny new objects are exciting and delicious, but the classics need our love just the same. If we all divert our attention away from them towards 'new things', we risk seeing those classics being sent to the sideline, which is very sad.

I hope you are excited to take your new knowledge out on your shopping trips or travels to expand on and develop your cheese palate.

I love to see people's cheese journeys, so please keep in touch with me via my Instagram @thecheeseexplorer and show me the cheeses you have discovered and the flavours you are identifying since reading this book.

Happy eating to you all!

Glossary

Here, you'll find a useful glossary for the more technical terms used in this book, and in the cheese world generally. Use them with enthusiasm to show off your cheese knowledge to all your family and friends.

ACIDIFICATION   Acidification is the first stage in cheesemaking. Lactic acid bacteria naturally present in milk or added in as starter cultures (see Cultures) convert the milk sugars (lactose) into lactic acid. Acidification starts the process of milk transforming into solids.

ACIDULANT   An acid that has been used in place of rennet or a coagulant. Lemon juice and vinegar are commonly used acidulants.

AFFINAGE   The refinement and maturing process.

AFFINEUR   A person who matures cheese.

ANNATTO   A natural dye added to cheese to make it orange.

AOP   L'Appellation d'origine protégée – the French equivalent of a PDO (see PDO).

BLUEING   The intentional addition and appearance of natural blue moulds on the surface or rind of a cheese.

BREAKDOWN   The softening of the texture of a cheese, predominantly seen beneath the rind.

CHEDDARING   A stage in the process of making Cheddar. The curds are formed into bricks and stacked on top of each other in piles to expel more whey and contribute to the final texture.

CHÈVRE	This is French for 'goat'. It is not a style of cheese. What is sometimes referred to as *'chevre'* is a fresh goats'-milk cheese.
COAGULANT	In cheesemaking, a coagulant separates liquid milk into solids (curds) and liquid (whey). Rennet (see Rennet) is a coagulant. The term 'coagulant' must be used for vegetarian, plant and microbial rennets, as rennet comes from an animal.
COAGULATION	The action of the proteins in milk forming together into a solid mass.
CULTURES	Bacteria that are naturally present in milk or selected and added into milk to start the acidification (see Acidification) process by producing lactic acid (see Lactic acid).
CURDS	The solids formed due to the process of coagulation.
DEACIDIFICATION	Deacidification refers to the alteration of the pH on the rind of a cheese. Lactic acid produced by the starter cultures is metabolised by yeasts, which increases the pH. This creates a surface that is more hospitable to desirable moulds.
DOP	Denominazione di Origine Protetta – the Italian equivalent of a PDO (see PDO).
DRAINAGE	An important stage in the cheesemaking process. Excess whey is drained from curds, either in moulds, cloths or removed topically, before a cheese can be made. Too much moisture and drainage issues can cause organoleptic and pathogenic problems.
FARMHOUSE	A cheese that has been made in the same location as the animals whose milk is used. In France this term, *'fermier'*, is stricter and refers to the size of the farm and the number of staff.

INOCULATION Inoculation in cheese refers to the introduction of strains of mould. This term is mainly used in blue cheesemaking for the *Penicillium* strains which are added in, inoculating the milk, and remain dormant until a later date.

LACTIC ACID BACTERIA LAB are the bacteria which acidify milk by creating lactic acid.

LACTOSE The natural sugar in milk.

MOULDS Fungi present on the rinds of certain cheeses. Also, containers that are used to form fresh curds into their final cheese shapes.

MUCOR A grey mould that is important in the character of cheeses such as Tomme de Savoie (page 102). It is disliked by many cheesemakers who are making fresh styles and it is notoriously difficult to eliminate in a dairy.

PASTA FILATA Literally translated from Italian as 'spun paste'. This term is used for cheeses which have had their curds stretched as part of the cheesemaking process. This applies to cheeses such as Mozzarella di Bufala Campana DOP (page 18) and Quesillo (page 21).

PASTE If a cheese has a rind, this refers to the middle, or anything which isn't rind. If a cheese is rindless, it refers to the whole mass.

PASTEURISATION The process of heating milk to a high temperature for a set amount of time. This kills off many bacteria which could be harmful in the cheesemaking process. It also kills many good bacteria.

PDO This stands for 'Protected Designation of Origin'. It is a UK and EU law to protect the tradition and geographical origin of cheeses and other food to promote the product and to eliminate imitations.

PGI This stands for 'Protected Geographical Indication', with a focus on the geographical location in which that product is made.

RAW MILK Milk that has not been heat-treated via pasteurisation (see Pasteurisation) or thermisation (see Thermisation).

RENNET An enzyme from a calf's stomach that is used to coagulate milk (see Coagulation).

RIND The exterior of a cheese. This can be natural, covered in moulds or washed. Some cheeses don't have rinds, for instance fresh cheeses or those aged in inorganic coatings such as wax.

THERMISATION A heat treatment of milk at a lower temperature than pasteurisation. This kills fewer bacteria than pasteurisation.

TRUCKLE A name referring to the shape of a cheese like a Cheddar. The shape has a flat top and bottom with a rounded perimeter.

UNPASTEURISED MILK Unpasteurised milk generally refers to milk that has not been subjected to heat treatment. It can, however, refer to milk which has been thermised but not pasteurised. For this book the term 'unpasteurised' refers to raw milk.

Thanks

Firstly, I would like to thank my family for all the support I have received over the time I have been working on this book. Mum and Sam, I am very grateful for the words of encouragement, dinners cooked and welcome distractions (some unwelcome, but you can't win them all) when I needed them most. There were a few points where you completely carried me, and I cannot thank you enough. Sam, your help with drinks matches also has been invaluable.

Also, to my extended family of rescue hens who are not only hilarious but also great therapy chickens.

Thank you to my friends for understanding why I have been less sociable and for putting up with my flakiness.

I'd like to thank my mum's friends Richard and Alison who allowed me to stay in their beachside chalet for extended visits to get away from distractions. I very much enjoyed hermit life with intermittent cold sea swims to wake me up and keep me energised.

Thank you to my peers in the cheese industry who helped with some of my decision-making processes. A special thank you to Jules Mons, Monika & Rupert Linton, Andy Swinscoe and Dave Holton.

A big thank you to the team at Ebury press, especially my editor Ru Merritt, who has been nothing but supportive for the entire process.

And finally, an enormous hug, kiss and thank you to all the cheesemakers, without whom my book would have no content.

Index

About the Author

Emma Young is a cheese specialist based in the UK. She teaches cheese retail courses for the Guild of Fine Food and is an accredited trainer for the Academy of Cheese, where she teaches in person in the UK and for overseas delegates. She has sold cheese at some of the leading cheese shops in the UK, including Mons Cheesemongers and Fine Cheese Company. When she isn't advising cheese businesses around the world, she is an international cheese judge and has judged for numerous competitions, including the World Cheese Awards, International Cheese Awards and many more. She can be found at cheeseexplorer.com or on Instagram @thecheeseexplorer.

Categories: herbaceous, fruit, malt, piquant, blue, sweet & nutty, umami, hard, spicy, semi-hard, animal, smoked, butter, acid, earth

Cheeses:
Gamonéu DOP
Castelmagno DOP
Bleu de Termignon
Cashel Blue
Fourme D'Ambert AOP
Leeds Blue
Montagnolo Affine
Gorgonzola Dolce DOP
Shropshire Blue
Blue Stilton PDO
Fourme de Montbrison AOP
Stichelton
Rogue River Blue
Bayley Hazen Blue
Lanark Blue
Cabrales DOP
Roquefort AOP
Emmentaler AOP
Mimolette
Beaufort AOP
Gouda
Comté AOP
Red Leicester
Le Gruyère AOP
Cheddar
Grana Padano DOP
Parmigiano Reggiano DOP
Deichkäse
São Jorge DOP
Lincolnshire Poacher
Provolone Valpadana DOP
Västerbottensost
Canastra
Dunbarton Blue
Manchego DOP
Sir iz mišine
Pecorino Sardo DOP
Cantal AOP
Salers AOP
Rauchkäse
Scamorza Affumicata
Chechil
Oscypek
Havarti
Asiago DOP
Lancashire
Oglesheld
Anster
Urstromshire
Old Roan
Caerphilly
Yorkshire Wensleydale PGI
Cheshire
Cornerstone
St Helena
Carraignamuc